Appalachian Magazine
March – May 2020

—*Presents*—

Spring has Sprung!

A collection of stories & articles highlighting the legends, travel destinations, history and lifestyle of Appalachia

Copyright © 2020 StatelyTies Media, dba Appalachian Magazine.

Volume 2, Issue 1

All rights reserved.

DEDICATION

James Alfred Fitzgerald
May 8, 1930—December 22, 2019
Known to my daughters simply as "Blue Papa" because he most often wore blue work shirts, "Blue Papa" was the embodiment of what it means to be an honorable Appalachian man. He loved to work. He loved his family. And he loved the God of Heaven.

Read more about Blue Papa on page 73

Appalachian Magazine is committed to serving as a living monument to the incredible lives of the men and women who call Appalachia home.

CONTENTS

Part One: Looking Back from Whence We've Come   **12**

Old Ways: Mountain Thoughts & Memories

Appalachian History

Mountain Religion

Featured – Buffalo Creek Disaster: 48 Years Later   30

Part Two: Living the Good Life   **64**

B&Bs, Trees, & Peas… Traveling Appalachia

Profiles & Heartwarming Stories

Featured – Blue Papa's Bible   73

Part Three: Straight Outta 'the Holler'   **84**

Appalachian Living, Healing, Growing & Eat'n

Tall Tales & Mountain Legends

Featured – Managing Snakes in a Residence, Business or Other Occupied Space   98

Part Four: Random Musings & My Two Cents   **108**

Featured – Does Appalachia Need a Flag?   120

"Spring Has Sprung"

Thank you for Subscribing to receive the Print Publication

On behalf of our family and partners, please allow me to sincerely say thank you for your purchase of *Appalachian Magazine*. We do not take lightly the fact that you have trusted us to present a year's worth of Appalachian stories to you.

You will notice that our publication is quite different than most other publications you may previously be accustomed to receiving – this is because we focus on providing content, free of cluttering advertisements.

When you purchase a subscription to our publication, your money is not going into the coffers of multimillion dollar publishing and media empires, but instead supports local families and an Appalachian-based small business!

Should you ever have any questions, desire to make an article submission or simply to say hello, we would love to hear from you! Send us an email at the following address:

TheMountainWriter@gmail.com

Also, check us out on social media:

Facebook.com/AppalachianMagazine

Instagram: AppalachianMagazine

YouTube: Appalachian Magazine

'Appalachian Magazine' is proud to be a family-owned small business.

Intro Photos to Each Section

Part One
Looking Back from Whence We've Come
The Elkhorn Church of God
Highsmith, C. M., photographer. (2015) Elkhorn, West Virginia, 2015.
Photograph retrieved from the Library of Congress,
https://www.loc.gov/item/2015634400/

Part Two
Living the Good Life
Sunday Afternoon Drive
Detroit Publishing Co., Publisher.
Old Man of the Mountain profile, White Mts., N.H. New Hampshire
[Between 1900 and 1915] Photograph.
https://www.loc.gov/item/2016814292/

Part Three
Straight Outta the 'Holler'
Dutton Calleb and his family with their homemade hoes
on the porch of their home near Knox County, Kentucky.
Wolcott, M. P., photographer. (November 1940) Photograph.
Retrieved from the Library of Congress,
https://www.loc.gov/item/2017805771/

Part Four
Random Musings & My Two Cents
Profile Lake and Old Man of the Mountain, White Mts., N.H. Cannon Mountain
Profile Lake and Old Man of the Mountain, White Mts., N.H. Detroit
Publishing Co., copyright claimant. [Between 1900 and 1920] Photograph.
https://www.loc.gov/item/2016796097/.

"Spring Has Sprung"

A note to our readers about the Coronavirus

At the time this book is being sent to the printers, March 17, 2020, the nation as we know it is in complete panic. Not a single one of the local stores in our community has toilet paper, canned food, Clorox, or even soap.

One month ago, the Dow Jones Industrial average was above 29,000 points, yesterday it closed at 20,188.52. Fears of a recession loom on the horizon and great uncertainty is in store.

The US death toll has risen to 85 and more than 4,600 people have tested positive for the virus. Churches, courts, schools and even sports are closing and no one knows what the future holds.

People are anxious and panicked. On one hand, the media is mocking people for clearing entire aisles at the grocery store of canned tuna, but on the other hand the incessant reporting from these very same people are the reason why so many of our friends and neighbors are panicked.

Like everyone else, we do not know what the future holds, this could all be a massive overreaction or things could become incomprehensibly worse by the time you receive this book.

With all of this being said, we wish to share with you a Facebook post we authored on Friday, March 13, 2020. It was true four days ago and we are confident that it will remain true:

In many respects, it feels like the world has gone crazy. Society has experienced far worse than the Coronavirus in days past and we'll certainly make it through this as well. In light of everything, we will make the following commitment to our readers: From this point forward, we will not report on anything virus related unless absolutely necessary and will instead focus on the great Appalachian stories people love… there are enough talking heads in the media as it is, we don't want to contribute to the overload of information… Thank you for supporting our publication. Be a good neighbor in the midst of this illness, take precautions, wash your hands and remember, this too shall pass.

We are a family owned and operated publication and our family loves each of you dearly and appreciate your continued support of 'Appalachian Magazine'.

—Part One—
Looking Back from Whence We've Come

"Spring Has Sprung"

—Part One—
Looking Back from Whence We've Come

Old Ways: Mountain Thoughts & Memories
Appalachia's Family Cemeteries – Pg. 14
Spring Houses: America's Earliest Refrigerators – Pg. 17
How to Read 'The Signs' for Planting and Hair Cutting – Pg.19
Jokes & Political Observations from July 1920 – Pg. 24

Appalachian History
Tour DuPont: Appalachia's Forgotten Bicycle Race– Pg. 26
100 Years After: The Battle of Matewan– Pg. 42
The Flying WV: How West Virginia's Most Iconic Symbol was Created – Pg. 51

—Featured—
Buffalo Creek Disaster: 48 Years Later – Pg. 30

Mountain Religion
Old Time Mountain Religion: Foot Washings – Pg. 59
High School Student: Who Controls Our Fate? – Pg. 61
The Confusing Process of Determining Easter's Date Each Year – Pg. 62
Was Jesus Crucified on a Wednesday? – Pg. 63

Appalachia's Family Cemeteries

As a child, my world was one spent somewhere between two mediums – the mountainous and free spirited hills of Southern West Virginia's coalfields and industrial Virginia.

Though I attended school in the Old Dominion, most of the life lessons I learned growing up occurred within the jagged borders of the Mountain State – it was there that I learned the value of family, heritage and the story of my ancestors. These traits grew to become defining principles I hope to not only exude in my own life, but to also pass down to my children.

To put it simply, people from the mountains are different and proud of it. They live differently, love differently and remember differently. They… We… cherish our remarkable and turbulent history. We were taught to appreciate the strength of our elders and grew to treasure the stories of bloody mine wars, hog killings, early settlers and grandma's pappy. In the mountains of Appalachia, history lives through the impoverished children who sat at their daddy's feet, listening to stories of brave men and women who gladly laid down their lives for the principle of a matter. Most early miners had nothing to leave to their children, nothing except for hundreds of stories and thousands of memories; yet these were the best inheritances any child could ever hope to receive.

It should then seem as no surprise that when it comes to disposing of our dead, we, in the hills of places like West Virginia, Kentucky and East Tennessee, do things far differently than most other Americans.

"Spring Has Sprung"

While the rest of the nation, by and large, lower their grandfathers beneath the dirt in a public cemetery – surrounded by hundreds or even thousands of strangers – West Virginians often return their fathers to plats of land that have been in the family's name for countless decades, maybe even centuries.

There, the very land of the family cemetery is sacred. For many, the thought of being buried anywhere other than alongside their brothers, parents, grandparents and earlier generations would be unthinkable.

Just outside of the town limits of the community of Delbarton, in Mingo County, West Virginia, my family has a consecrated piece of ground that has been the site of countless tears, yet holds a dear place in the hearts of all of us who share a common name and common heritage – it is the Farley Family Cemetery. It's not the only family cemetery alongside the winding stream known as Elk Creek – in fact there are a countless number of family burial sites throughout the valley, but this one is ours.

It is the only location on earth I have ever witnessed my father shed tears. It is the only site where I can come within a few feet of my great-great-great grandfather. It is the most sacred spot in the world for our family, yet there are thousands just like it throughout West Virginia alone. These are family cemeteries and they're as much a part of life in Appalachia as moonshine and churchgoing.

As the Virginia pioneers pushed farther west, they encountered a world that was isolated, rugged and a place where death's cold shadow could be lurking behind every passing turn. Times were hard, but these men and women were resilient and they pressed on – undeterred by the sting of their own mortality.

As a matter of practicality, during the early years of Western Virginia's history, families would clear out a small plot of land, often in wooded areas bordering their fields, and bury a child that had succumbed to a fever or persistent cough. Next, an uncle would be buried alongside the child. Then a second child would be buried, followed by mother and father.

For the surviving children, these hallowed acres was the site of pain, maturity and the realization that life is indeed fragile — to put it simply, that piece of ground defined them.

As they grew older, they cherished those old burial sites, painstakingly mowing the sites, managing additional plots and working to ensure their children were grossly aware of the story each of the cold headstones told.

The remnants of these centuries old cemeteries are still visible today, often just a few yards from the old family home place.

For our family, like so many others, the family cemetery remains a critical component of who we are and each time a family member dies, there is never a question regarding where that person will be buried.

Sadly, those old men who dedicated so many hours to maintaining the gardens of the dead — many of which have graves marked only by concrete (marble was too costly for many early families), have now joined their mothers and fathers beneath the soil in those same hallowed resting places.

With their passing, the question remains, "Who's going to fill their shoes?" Who will step in and continue the work that had been passed down to them? Who in the 21st century even has time to do this?

These are very good questions and as this writer drives through the mountains of Appalachia and sees so many grave sites and family cemeteries growing over, he can't help but answer, "very few."

Spring Houses: America's Earliest Refrigerators

Photo: *A spring house near Collegeville, Pennsylvania. Courtesy of Michael H. Parker*

For many of us, it's hard not to imagine a time prior to running water and refrigeration. The availability of reliable and clean drinking water every day or the luxury of enjoying a cold glass of milk on a hot summers afternoon were a luxury not enjoyed by many even as recently as a century ago.

Thanks to an ingenious and simple solution, however, a countless number of American households had their entire quality of life elevated with the implementation of a basic structure that came to be known as a spring house.

Dating back to the days of Christ, the concept of a spring house is relatively straightforward: A small building, usually nothing more than a single tiny room, would be constructed over a spring or small creek.

As pioneers pushed westward and Appalachia became settled – one hollow at a time – the predominance of mountain spring houses also increased.

Originally, the purpose of a spring house was to keep the spring water clean by protecting it from fallen leaves or dead animals; however, settlers soon found that by enclosing a structure around a chilly mountain stream, the temperature inside the spring house also dramatically decreased.

This allowed for something revolutionary – enclosed refrigeration.

Before the advent of electric refrigeration or ice delivery, settlers and mountain families were storing food that would otherwise spoil inside their spring houses. Packing the buildings with meat, fruit and dairy products.

In order to keep away hungry scavengers and other wildlife such as bear or mountain lions, stone became the building material of choice for Appalachian spring houses.

In 1881, Harvard educated botanist and plant pathologist Byron David Halsted, published the book, *Barn Plans and Outbuildings*. The book's purpose was provide American farmers with the outlines and blueprints necessary for building essential buildings for a rural homeplace. Halsted dedicated an entire chapter to spring houses, writing, "The main points to look at in constructing a spring house are coolness of water, purity of air, the preservation of an even temperature during all seasons, and perfect drainage."

Barn Plans and Outbuildings, published 1881
Written by Byron David Halsted

Coolness of water is realized by conducting the water through pipes placed at least four feet underground. The New York writer advised, "The spring should be dug out and cleaned and the sides evenly built up with rough stone work. The top should be arched over or shaded from the sun. A spout from the spring carries the water into the house. If the spring is sufficiently high, it would be most convenient to have the water trough in the house elevated upon a bench… There is then no necessity for stooping to place the pans in the water or to take them out. Where the spring is too low for this, the trough may be made on a level with the floor.

The purity of the air was "Secured by removing all stagnant water or filth from around the spring. All decaying roots and muck that may have collected should be removed and the ground around the house either paved roughly with stone or sodded. The openings which admit and discharge the water should be large enough to allow a free current of air to pass in or out. These openings are to be covered with wire gauze to prevent insects or vermin from entering the house. The house should be smoothly plastered and frequently whitewashed with lime and a large ventilator should be made in the ceiling. There should be no wood used in the walls or floors or water channels.

An even temperature can best be secured by building of stone or brick with walls twelve inches thick, double windows, and a *ceiled* roof. In such a house there will be no danger of freezing in the winter time.

The drainage will be secured by choosing the site so that there is ample fall for the waste water.

How to Read 'The Signs' for Planting and Hair Cutting

"And God said, Let there be lights in the firmament of the heaven to divide the day from the night; and let them be for signs, and for seasons, and for days, and years... And God made two great lights; the greater light to rule the day, and the lesser light to rule the night: he made the stars also."

These are the words found in Genesis chapter one. They tell of how the God of heaven established lights in the sky, the sun, moon and stars. At first glance, many modern readers may skim right past a five-word phrase concerning these astrological bodies; however, a century or more ago, this particular phrase dominated the lives of countless Americans: "...let them be for signs..."

As a child, I have heard about "the signs" my whole life.

Even today, several decades after the fact, I can still hear my great-grandmother's shaky voice like it was yesterday, "You need to get your taters in the ground tomorrow, 'cause the signs is right'."

The last "Granny Woman" of our family, my 'Mamaw' served as a wealth of knowledge for most everything we encountered in our Appalachian community, and in the springtime, folks from all over the holler would come seeking her advice regarding when to plant their gardens. She was a firm believer in "planting by the signs".

Described as devilish by some and extolled by others; I never truly understood what any of it meant until long after she was gone, but as I age, I find myself becoming more and more fascinated by the complex astrological system she relied upon for the better part of a century.

Today, most everyone who plants a garden does so as a mere hobby or at the very most in an effort to supplement their grocery store purchases; however, 150 years ago, a successful garden was often the difference between surviving the winter and starving to death.

As a result, the folks "back in the day" took a far more serious approach to planting and the moon's phases helped to serve as a guide to improve their chances of a successful garden.

In its simplest of forms, "planting by the signs" means that you plant crops that will produce their fruits above the ground during the waxing moon (the time between a new moon and a full moon — when the moon is getting bigger), while plants that produce their crop below the ground must be planted during a waning moon (the time between a full moon and a new moon — when the moon is shrinking).

Lori Elliott, writes, "Many old-time farmers also planted and harvested by the astrological signs. Barren signs, such as Aquarius, Gemini, and Leo, would have been considered ideal times for plowing and cultivating the soil, while fertile signs such as Cancer, Scorpio, and Pisces would have been considered the best times for planting seeds."

The West Virginia Commissioner of Agriculture published the following guide to planting by the signs:

There are many people who scoff at the idea of using the signs of the Zodiac and the moon to garden. But, there are also many who use this method even though they don't talk about it, as though it was something to be ashamed of. It just isn't modern and scientific enough for this technological age of chemical food and insecticides. Yet, if one will take the time to read or listen, one will discover that the times to plant, rototill, spray, etc., touted by the "experts," matches almost to the day the old timers' method of planting by the signs.

The use of the signs goes back beyond recorded history. Its really quite incredible that the use of the signs has survived. Basically there are two ways of looking at the moon – the sun phases and the zodiac phases. Let's look at them individually.

The Sun Phases

The sun phases describe the way the sun shines on the moon as seen from planet earth. These phases are also called quarters, and there are four quarters as the moon goes around the earth. The first quarter begins with the new moon which occurs when the moon is between the earth and the sun and is totally dark as viewed from the earth.

As the moon (month) proceeds, it becomes visible in the shape of a crescent until it is half visible; this is the end of the first quarter and the start of the second. The second quarter proceeds until the moon is a totally visible circular pie, and we have a full moon which is the end of the second quarter and the start of the third.

Continuing, the moon now begins to darken on one side until it is again a half moon; we have the end of the third quarter and the start of the fourth. The fourth quarter occurs from this point and is again a crescent until the new moon.

The Zodiac Phases

Now for the zodiac phases. The moon, as it travels around the earth, passes through 12 sectors named after the familiar signs of the zodiac. Each sector is associated with a group of stars discovered by the ancients and called constellations. These constellations are in turn associated with parts of the body and other qualities. The part of the body governed by an individual constellation is supposed to be more sensitive when the moon is in that constellation. The moon goes through each constellation at least once each month and is in a constellation for either two or three days at a time.

How Do You Know?

The way you know which constellation and which quarter of the moon is in, is by your trusty planting calendar. Rush down to your local hardware, auto, seed, and/or feed store and see if you can get a freebie. The zodiac signs and moon phase signs are clearly marked.

What Do You Do With It?

Now we get to the nitty gritty. You have two sets of instructions; ideally you should consult both before planting. For instance, you should plant during one of the fruitful signs of the zodiac and the appropriate quarter of the moon.

The Signs Of The Zodiac

The signs of the zodiac are listed starting below and continued on the following page along with the qualities of the signs. In general, plant during the moist and fruitful signs and do things that require dryness (burning and destroying weeds) during the dry signs. The most fruitful signs are Cancer, Taurus, Scorpio and Pisces. The barren signs are Aries, Sagittarius, Gemini, Leo, Virgo and Aquarius. One more point: never plant or graft on the sun's day (Sunday) for it is a barren hot day.

ARIES (head & face): Dry and barren. Never plant. Best sign for plowing, tilling and cultivating. TAURUS (neck): Earthy and moist. Plant here to withstand a drought. Excellent for root crops and okay for crops above the ground and flowers. GEMINI (arms): Airy, dry and barren. Destroy weeds, kill trees and prepare soil.

CANCER (breast): Watery and very fruitful. Plant here to withstand a drought. Excellent for above and below-ground crops. Time to graft.

LEO (head): Fiery, dry and barren. Never plant; destroy weeds, kill trees and prepare soil.

VIRGO (bowels): Earthy, dry and barren. Destroy weeds, kill trees and prepare soil.

LIBRA (balance): Airy, moist and semi fruitful. Excellent for flowers (beauty) and okay for above-ground crops.

SCORPIO (loins): Watery and fruitful. Excellent for above ground crops and flowers. Okay for below-ground crops. Time to graft.

SAGITTARIUS (thighs): Fiery, dry, and barren. Destroy weeds and kill trees.

CAPRICORN (knees): Earthy, moist and productive. Good for root crops and okay for above ground crops. Root cuttings and make grafts.

AQUARIUS (legs): Airy, dry and barren. Destroy weeds and kill trees.

PISCES (feet): Watery and fruitful. Plant here to withstand a drought. Excellent for below ground crops and okay for above ground crops. Root cuttings and make grafts.

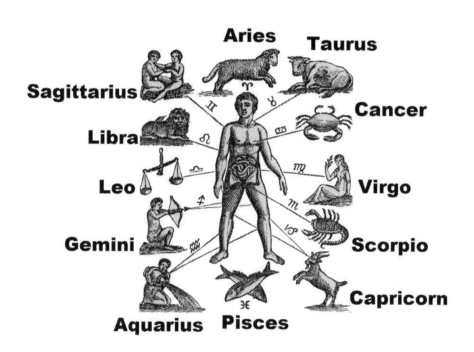

Old timers lived by these signs for centuries, but the one question remains: is there any science to back up their traditions?

Twenty-five years ago, the *New York Times* set out to determine if planting by the full moon was a bright idea or lunacy; unfortunately, they were not able to reach any definitive conclusions.

Scientists at NASA stated that planting by the moon was pure "mythology" and nothing more; however, Dr. Mac Cathey Ph.D. in plant physiology, told the *Times* that his grandmother gardened by the signs in North Carolina. "And she was a tremendous gardener... But all our high-germinating seeds and pesticides have damped out our ability to read the signs... It's like music. We can't sight-read anymore."

Regardless of whether you're a believer or not, chances are the folks in your family tree religiously planted by the signs only a few generations ago.

The Signs Ain't Just for Planting!

"G'ma and Dad always did everything based on the signs! Oh yes, it works! For potty-training and weaning from bottle, also for cutting hair at the right date to make it grow slower or faster. Our God made our bodies and the earth to be in sync..." wrote one *Appalachian Magazine* reader when asked if signs work.

If you're thinking that cutting one's hair based upon the phases moon is some archaic relic of Appalachian mountain lore, you might be shocked to learn that the writers at *Glamour* explored this topic a few years after one of the individuals serving in their "Girls in the Beauty Department" was thumbing through a *Farmers' Almanac* and came upon a lists for the "best dates for cutting hair to increase growth, right alongside its suggested dates for planting crops or mowing the lawn."

Sandi Duncan, managing editor for *Farmers Almanac* kindly explained to fashion writer Petra Guglielmetti the back story behind such a belief:

"Many people believe that the moon has a direct pull not only on the tides, but a variety of other living things on earth."

Including hair.

Schwarzkopf International, an international brand that offers tips for the care of one's hair, had this to say:

"Conditions during the waxing moon promote hair growth after a haircut. Therefore, you should cut your hair between the new and full moon if you want your hair to grow fast after a haircut. If you wear short hair and you want your hair to grow as slowly as possible you should cut your hair during the waning phase of the moon (between the full and new moon). Your short hairstyle will keep its shape longer."

Jokes & Political Observations from July 1920

The following are a list of jokes published in the July 1920 edition of "The Retail Coalman". A Pennsylvania-based publication dedicated to covering the coal industry.

THE POOR FARMER
The farmer will never be completely happy until he can sell his wheat at the 1920 price and still hire his hands at the 1890 wage.

THE SWITCHMEN
The switchmen seem to have the idea that the way to bring heaven nearer earth is to raise hell.

SAFETY FIRST
Reporter: And what are you for in the present campaign?
Candidate: I am for anything that nobody is against!

ADVICE
There is a lot of advice given us because somebody wants to see how it would come out and doesn't want to take a chance himself.

WE DON'T SEE SERPENTS LIKE WE USED TO
Another thing that prohibition has done is to cut down the number of sea serpents seen at the summer resorts.

SEE THE POINT: Union Workers
Sam, the colored driver of an ox team saw a little lizard crawling up a tree. He flourished his long whip and very deftly snapped off the lizard's head. Further along the road, with skillful precision, he picked a horse fly off the fence with the same weapon. His skill as a marksman was next exhibited on a chipmunk that showed its head above the ground. The white man said, "Sam, take a crack at that, pointing at a hornet's nest." Sam grinned and replied, "No sir, no sir, boss. Them fella's is organized!"

"Spring Has Sprung"

Autocar saves time and money wherever there is coal to be hauled

Autocar
Wherever there's a road

HAVE YOU GRAY HAIR?

Van's Mexican Hair Restorative will restore it to its perfect natural color. This we positively guarantee. It will remove all Dandruff, heal all sores, stop Hair from Falling Out. Cures Baldness where it is possible to be done, and cools the head and brains. It is no dye, and is warranted absolutely free from Sugar of Lead or anything injurious whatever. Money refunded if it does not do everything that is claimed for it. Sent to any address on receipt of price. Full information free. $1 per Bottle.
AGENTS WANTED.   Address   818918

Mention this paper   ALLEN & CO., Room 312, Inter-Ocean Building, CHICAGO, ILL.

Belmont College,
...NASHVILLE, TENN...

REV. R. A. YOUNG, D.D., Regent.   MISS HOOD, MISS HERON, Principals.

The Ideal College
Home of the South.

Tour DuPont
Appalachia's Forgotten Bicycle Race

I attended elementary school in the early 1990s in Wytheville, Virginia. It seemed like each spring our class would spend an entire week putting together homemade signs and gathering American flags for an event that always signified the much awaited summer break wasn't too far off.

After all of our work creating signs was complete, one random May morning we would gather onto the yellow county-owned school busses and ride to the town's downtown district – cheering on the American cyclists in an event few Americans even know ever existed, but one that I will never forget: the Tour DuPont.

For a young farm kid growing up in a rural mountain community, the annual bicycle race offered me and the rest of the kids in our tiny town a rare gem seldom afforded to Southwest Virginians – the opportunity to participate in an international event. And best of all, it took place right in front of Skeeters, the local hometown hotdog joint.

For me the day was always special, as it brought in so many sights and sounds that were not normal for our mountain community. There were Japanese, Norwegian, British and French flags being waved by people who spoke with funny accents and in foreign languages. It was the biggest thing my young eyes had ever seen.

Unfortunately, the Tour DuPont ran its final race in 1996 and from my vantage point, it seemed like nearly everyone in my town, and the nation as a whole, seemingly forgot about this annual event.

A few months ago, some 24 years following the event's final race, I sat out to research whatever happened to the Tour DuPont, as well as learn more about what got the whole thing started and I was astonished by what I found.

For starters, my first surprise was to learn that the race was not started as the "Tour DuPont" but initially as the "Tour de Trump", named after a rather unassuming guy you may have heard of before… Donald J. Trump!

The idea for the race was conceived by CBS Sports reporter John Tesh, who had covered the 1987 Tour de France and on his return suggested holding a race in the United States to the basketball commentator and entrepreneur Billy Packer. Packer originally planned to call the race the Tour de Jersey and approached representatives of casinos in Atlantic City for sponsorship, and Trump offered to be the race's primary sponsor and the Tour de Trump became a thing.

The total prize money for the first event in 1989 was a quarter million dollars, including $50,000 for the winner.

This, together with the race's place in the international calendar

"Spring Has Sprung"

between the Giro d'Italia and the Tour de France, made it attractive to high-profile riders and teams, but the event did not attract large crowds.

Interviewed on NBC prior to the start of the 1989 race, Trump stated that "I would like to make this the equivalent of the Tour de France."

The inaugural Tour de Trump started in Albany, New York, and consisted of 10 stages, totaling 837 miles, taking in five Eastern states.

The route took the race south from Albany to Richmond, Virginia, and then across to Atlantic City, where it finished in front of Trump's casino.

The 1989 race was won by the Norwegian rider Dag Otto Lauritzen of the American team 7-Eleven.

Photo: *1989 Tour de Trump cycle race, Richmond, Virginia, USA. Photo courtesy of Donald West from Richmond, Virginia, United States of America.*

In 1991, American chemical manufacturer DuPont signed on as the race's title sponsor and the event was renamed "Tour DuPont."

In the years that followed, the race's course changed multiple times; however, every event passed through Richmond, Virginia.

During its six years as the Tour DuPont, the race was won by Dutch rider Erik Breukink, Greg LeMond, Raúl Alcalá, Russian Viatcheslav Ekimov, and twice by American Lance Armstrong. I still remember standing in line to get the autograph from a little known cyclist named Lance Armstrong... and I sure do wish I still had that signed paper program.

School would always let out early on Tour DuPont days, as soon as the cyclists raced out of sight on Main Street and without fail, every free minute of the next week would have me racing my red Huffy bike up and down our gravel farm road competing – if only in my mind – against the dozens of men from all over the world I had seen race out of sight of my Wytheville, Virginia.

Photo: Pre-race festivities leading up to the Tour Dupont in Wytheville, Virginia. Courtesy of Town of Wytheville.

Sadly, all good things must come to an end and in July 1996, DuPont announced that it was ending its sponsorship of the race. According to a brand manager for the company, "Over the past six years, the Tour DuPont has been an excellent vehicle for promoting our products. However, we need to focus more on strategic markets in other parts of the world, where a sustained annual program versus a two-week event can better leverage the DuPont brand equity for profitable growth".

Historian Eric Reed notes that a DuPont marketing executive characterized the initial sponsorship as "a bargain", and that the company claimed that the American press clippings generated by the event weighed 29 pounds. DuPont executives also reported that they valued the global media exposure as worth close to $70 million.

Reed quotes a DuPont marketing executive as stating: "In 40 years in [media relations], I have never seen such concentrated, sustained and positive media coverage". However, Reed argues that despite this initial enthusiasm, "the Tour DuPont's chronic weaknesses hamstrung the event's growth", citing its "pro-am" status, which prevented professional riders from being able to win world ranking points in the event.

He also states that despite having an estimated worldwide television audience of 200 million, "American fan enthusiasm and roadside spectator interest in the event failed to spike significantly."

After DuPont's withdrawal, race organizers tentatively scheduled a 1997 race and even considered expanding the event as a triple crown – multi-continent race, competing in China (Asia), United States (North America) and concluding with the Tour de France (Europe), but these plans were never realized and the race was discontinued altogether.

Though plans of the race rivaling the Tour de France were never realized, the race did succeed in broadening at least one Appalachian child's understanding of the world and provided an opportunity for me to dream. Though forgotten by so many, I for one will never forget the Tour DuPont.

—*Featured*—
Buffalo Creek Disaster: 48 Years Later

This article was made possible by contributions from Appalachian Magazine, Richard Roche, Daily Kos, and Marshall University Library and the depositions of flood victims.

Saturday, February 26, 1972, was a day Logan County, West Virginia, resident, Tom Sparks, never forgot.

For Sparks, the morning began in the wee hours of night. Tossing and turning in his bed, the West Virginia man grew increasingly fearful of the potential danger the past week's rain deluge was placing upon his home, family and neighbors.

Sparks' fears were not baseless. His family lived just yards below a series of makeshift dams that had been constructed to store nearly three decades' worth of mine sludge—the liquid and solid waste byproduct that results from the coal mining process.

February 1972's rainfall levels totaled to an astonishing amount that was 86% greater than the month's average reading. This fact, coupled with the understanding that deep mountaintop snows were beginning to melt caused an uneasy tension to sweep through the communities downstream of an unstable chain of dams constructed by mining companies.

Despite these fears, very few residents chose to leave their homes — a move that would prove devastating in the coming hours.

Unable to sleep, Sparks gathered his family together around 3 a.m. and headed to Bernie Wilson's home, where they would be safer.

Wilson was a family friend who, like Sparks, believed the dam was approaching disastrous levels.

Shortly after daybreak, Sparks and Wilson left the residence and headed to a nearby service station to purchase gasoline. Afterwards, they picked up Harold Sloane, a mutual friend, and drove to Sparks' house where the group began feeding hogs.

Just yards below the dam, Sparks entered the cramped and narrow hog pen. Wilson and Sloane leaned against the enclosure, talking to him as he performed his daily chores.

In a matter of moments, the morning's foggy serenity vanished, as the men heard the undeniable sound of water rushing over the dam.

Looking to the top of the mountain, Sloan and Wilson observed a charging wall of mine sludge racing their way.

Notes from an interview with the men, taken roughly a month later, declared:

"He saw the water hit... on the outside of the dam, approximately 100 yards from Sparks' house, across the road at the right of the dam. Mr. Wilson said the slag dump exploded, carrying water and slag 100 feet in the air."

"The water coming over the dam pitched up and shifted to the right side of the dam," said Wilson, who yelled for the men to get away from the hog house and run to higher ground.

"All three men ran across the highway, over the railroad tracks and up the mountain directly opposite Sparks' house."

Unable to do anything but watch the destruction unfold, the men looked on from the side of the mountain as more than 130

MILLION gallons of black wastewater roared through the valley.

First to be wiped out was the community's church, located just below the series of dams.

The wall of death then continued down the hillside, taking out Harold Sloane's house.

Charging through the valley, thirty years' worth of polluted water destroyed the pig pen the men had just been gathered around, before sweeping Sparks' home and vehicles down the valley.

In the seconds that followed, the State of West Virginia would experience the worst flood in its history and the same county that played host to a deadly stand-off between striking miners and armed mine bosses—roughly a half century earlier— would soon find itself embroiled in yet another struggle between the residents of the mountains and the mega-corporations that owned the mineral rights beneath their feet.

In total, sixteen West Virginia communities were devastated by the flood, leaving 5,000 individuals home-less, 1,121 injured and at least 125 people dead.

The Genesis of a Tragedy

The origins of the Buffalo Creek catastrophe can be traced directly to the late-1940s, which saw an industrial boom as the nation transformed its war efforts to peacetime manufacturing.

It was in this decade that the Lorado Coal Mining Company opened Mine No. 5 near the top of Buffalo Hollow, just upstream of Saunders, West Virginia.

Unaware of the problems that would be created by their actions nearly thirty years later, company officials completed the Mine No. 5 preparation plant in 1947 and began dumping refuse near the intersection of Middle Fork and Buffalo Creek, amounting to roughly 1,000 tons per day.

The refuse, known as coal slurry, was comprised of solid and liquid waste that is a by-product of the coal mining process.

It wasn't until the 1950s that state leaders began to recognize the impact this practice was having on its fresh water streams and rivers, mostly as they related to fish and wildlife.

In the years ahead, West Virginia officials ordered the practice of discharging coal waste directly into waterways to be discontinued. In the process of doing this, however, another problem was created: What to do with the waste water?

Initially, it was decided to pump the wastewater into abandoned mines and holding ponds above ground.

Then, in the early 1960s, the mining company decided to build a dam across Middle Fork Creek – which discharged into Buffalo Creek at Saunders – this became known as dam number one.

More than likely, the building of dam number one on the Middle Fork was looked at as an ingenious move. Not only was the coal slurry contained behind the dam, but the dam itself acted as a filter – with clean water seeping out the opposite downstream side.

Approval was granted for this "new" method of disposing of the coal waste, although no known study was ever performed relating to the impact this new method would have if the dam ever broke.

Thus, the stage was being set for one of America's worst industrial disasters to date – *it should be noted that the Great Johnstown Flood of 1889 in Pennsylvania killed over 2,000 people. The 1889 incident also included a man-made dam bursting.*

A Danger is Compounded

In the late 1960s, the holding area behind dam number one became full of sold refuse and silt from the previous decade. Though water still trickled through the dam, the holding area was no longer large enough for the amount of waste being dumped into it, so a simple solution was devised: Build another dam.

Dam number two was built back, farther upstream, and the mining operation continued at Buffalo Creek.

Richard M. Roche is a supervising inspector for the New York City Fire Department and president of Roche Group, a consulting firm that provides management and training services to companies that do business in the coal industry.

Describing the second dam's construction, Roche stated, "little thought was put into the impact that failure of these dams would have on the communities below and it's very doubtful that much scientific engineering was put into the whole matter either."

With the mine at Buffalo Creek continuing in full operation, times were good. Miners were making satisfactory wages, coal companies were getting wealthy and no questions were really asked. Any questions that were being raised by coal officials and government leaders had nothing to do with dams breaking. The safety concerns of most in the industry at that time were focused on how to prevent explosions and fires in the mines themselves, which were far too common throughout the nation's coal mines.

By October 1966, the mine had been purchased by a new company, Buffalo Creek Mining Company, which continued the practice of damming the valley with mining byproducts.

That same month, a dam with a very similar design and function burst at a coal mine in Wales, United Kingdom, realizing a huge mass of liquefied coal waste.

Concerned that something similar to the Wales incident might occur in the United States, the US Bureau of Mines prepared a list of similar waste banks in the Appalachian coal mining region and began the process of inspecting each of them, fearful that their "failure could result in loss of life or extensive property damage."

Shortly after this event, the UMW District Office asked local offices to send any information on unsafe conditions in their area. Frank Brown, recording secretary of the local union at Lorado, sent a letter to the district president, advising him of the danger from the dams on Buffalo Creek. In 1968, dam number three was begun even farther upstream and was completed in the following decade.

The Experts Weigh In

Richard M. Roche was a major contributor to this article. In his submitted work, Roche writes, "I would like to bring two interesting points our here. First, when would this stop? Are we to believe that after dam number three they would have built a dam four and so on and so on? Did the coal company figure they could continue to build dams, avert any disaster, and by the time the coal ran out they would just close up the mine and move on? Leaving billions of gallons of coal waste behind?

"Second, how could no one at this point say, 'wait a minute, we can't do this! If these dams fail, for whatever reason, Buffalo Creek's communities will be wiped out all the way to the Guyandotte River at the City of Man.' I find it almost unbelievable, but things went on – business as usual.

"By the time of the disaster, the water and waste in dam number three towered 250 feet above Saunders, at the mouth where Middle Fork dumped into Buffalo Creek, and over 130 million gallons of water were contained behind the dams. It is only fair for me to say that various concerned citizens voiced their opinions of concern on and off, but no action seemed to have been taken."

By 1970, the mine's ownership had once again transferred hands, this time to Pittston Coal Company, a large mining corporation.

According to Dennis Deiz, the network of sledge dams completely blocked the streams from their natural course.

The Eleventh Hour

Roche writes, "It would be very easy for one to start casting blame at individuals at this point, as many stories of eleventh hour calls of concern to officials and law enforcement agencies, wives nagging at husbands to leave the area until the rains stopped are told to this day.

"In reality, one man could have changed the whole outcome and he did not. In fact, for reasons only he would ever be able to say, if he were still alive, he simply got into his car and quickly left the area, heading back to New York. He was the most powerful coal official on the scene and he could have easily made a call to the state police and requested an evacuation of the area be started; instead, he did nothing.

"Again, in fairness to all those involved in the eleventh hour before the disaster, they most likely had no real idea what to do. They were police officers, businessmen, coal miners, and yes, wives and girlfriends, not dam builders and engineers, and certainly not Mother Nature. The truth is the dice had been cast for this tragedy back in the 1940s, when coal mining began up Buffalo Creek in Saunders.

"When they started building dams, additional die were cast and all along without the thought of impact – the impact on the region and more specifically, the impact on the helpless citizens of Buffalo Creek, West Virginia.

The Day of Reckoning

Saturday, February 26, 1972, proved to be a day of reckoning, as the laws of nature came to collect a debt owed to it by the coal companies who had operated the series dams blocking Buffalo Creek.

Sadly, the unbearable payment would be made by the citizens of West Virginia, as 125 people paid with their lives. Thousands of homes would be destroyed in a single instance and even more individuals would be forever marked by the scars of such tragedy.

Ezra Lusk lived below the dam and was at her home the morning the dams burst.

Protected by a rolling hill, Lusk's home was never impacted by the flood of water.

Hearing the deafening sounds of the dam from her porch, Lusk watched as a boy ran to safety atop the crest of the hill in front of her house.

Telling her story to investigators two months following the flood, Lusk stated, "There was a boy come running off the hill and said, 'everything is gone.' I said 'what do you mean everything gone,' and he said, 'there ain't nothing down there, church house or nothing' But, it was hard for me to believe that, so I just went on down to see, and there wasn't…"

Carol Hoosier was a Logan County housewife, whose husband was an employee of the Buffalo Mining Company.

According to her testimony, Hoosier overheard someone telling her husband, who was sitting on their front porch, that the dam was about to break.

At this point, she decided to warn her parents who lived next door.

Entering her parent's house, she quickly warned her mother, who was in the kitchen and her father, who was still in bed.

She later stated that her father became mad and told her "not to become upset over nothing."

No sooner than returning to the kitchen, Hoosier heard a loud noise which sounded like boards banging together.

Looking out the kitchen door, she observed water and debris rushing toward the house.

Yelling from across the road, Hoosier's husband directed her to get in their car and drive the couple's two children to safety up a mine road.

Running out the door, Hoosier said that she watched as her mother went into the bedroom to get her father.

She, her husband, and children jumped in the family's automobile and raced to safety, while debris rubbed against the rear of the car.

Sadly, Hoosier said her mother and father never left their house, which was washed away in the flood. Upon reaching safety, the young mother looked back and could see a wall of black water covering the entire hollow.

The trauma felt by the Hoosiers and Mrs. Lusk was shared by thousands others that day, including Evelyn Juanita Fields, "So when my father got back he and my mother were just standing there watching the creek. We still hadn't got out of the house or anything because we didn't believe it.

Then he made us get in the car and took us up Proctor Hollow to park the car out of the way of the water.

"We came back down to the store to watch, to see if the water would get up. When we got down there my mother made me go in the store and buy a big jacket because it was real cold that morning and after I came back out my mother had remembered the little boy – his mother had taken him to the house next door –because she and her husband were separated and she had taken him to the house the night before to spend the night there.

"My mother was afraid she had her other little children there, so she sent my father back to tell her to get out and warn her about it.

"So when my father got up to the bridge, me and my mother were standing there at the foot of the steps at the store and we could look straight up the road and see our house and all the other houses in the bottom where we live.

"My mother had turned around or something and I was looking up there – by this time my father had seen the water coming when he got to the bridge – he didn't get to go to that house. He turned around and started running back. I looked up there and saw our house move. It just picked up and moved over next to our next-door neighbor's house and that's all I remember seeing because it seems like I just went deaf completely.

"I couldn't hear, I couldn't see, I couldn't do anything. I stood there screaming and that's when my mother saw the house moving. My father grabbed me and my mother and my cousin came down there with us too, and my father made her get in the car and come with us.

"My father made us start up Proctor Hollow. He had to drag my mother. He pulled her up Proctor Hollow and when we started running up the hollow the power lines and things started breaking and I was almost up to our car then. But my father had to drag my mother back down the hollow away from the wires so they would not fall on her and before they fell completely to the road, they quit breaking.

"By this time, we made it completely up to our car. My father said he could hear the screaming and houses breaking, but I didn't hear anything – I was completely deaf. I could hear nothing."

The Impact of the Tragedy
Richard M. Roche:

Today, over 40 years later, Buffalo Creek is very different. There are those that say things never returned to what they were after the February 1972 flood, and how could they? The whole valley and communities were obliterated off the map; victim to the impact of the disaster in two ways, physically and geographically.

I am often asked could this ever happen again?

My answer is this: It will never happen again in Buffalo Creek, West Virginia, and I do not believe that it will happen again in this way or in this country. But yes, I do believe it could in some land where ideas turn to reality overnight, before any thought is given to the impact that idea may have. For instance, not too long ago, in Turkey a horrific coal mine fire killed countless hundreds; why? Because history repeats itself if we don't learn from it and unfortunately, it seems that no one there bothered to take the time to learn from the US coal industry at how to minimize coal mine fires and explosions; things we learned long ago in this country.

In fact, to a great degree, what we did not learn from the British coal industry, we learned the hard way, through trial, error and tragedy.

The Buffalo Creek coal industry disaster has left a lasting impact on not only me, but countless hundreds… no thousands… that were impacted in some way by the disaster.

With each year we go further away from this tragedy, we lose not only survivors of that terrible day, but others, like me, who have researched the event and sought its deeper lessons and meanings.

Someday, there will be no one left that was alive that day in February 1972, and only our writings and recollections of the even put on paper will remain for generations to come to learn from.

We can only hope and pray that perhaps the impact this event had on our lives will prevent similar tragedies from impacting others' lives after we are long gone. If we can achieve that we perhaps, just perhaps, can put a positive spin on an otherwise senseless tragedy.

In Their Words, Courtesy of Daily Kos

Barbara Elkins was 7 when the flood happened, and she and her two sisters lost their mother:

"We ran to the back door, but the water was already on the front steps. Dad tried to get us up to the loft. He tried to get mommy up there but he couldn't. He was putting her up there, and then the house just came down like toothpicks. We all just started drifting with the water. We were all hanging onto Daddy, and this big old car came and hit Daddy in the side and knocked Mommy loose from him. And I was hanging onto her. Me and Mom got separated.

"Daddy had those two," Barbara said, pointing to her sisters. "He found a little bank and put them on it. The last time we saw Mommy, she was going down the river hollering for help."

Carol Hoosier: "I still can't sleep when it rains."

Yale sociologist Kai Erickson wrote a book about the impact of the flood on the lives and psyches of the survivors, entitled "Everything in its Path." He described the psychic trauma that afflicted the survivors as a kind of "disaster syndrome", and survivors' guilt was one of its characteristics.

Those who lived in the winding hollow formed by Buffalo Creek often survived merely due to which side of the creek their house was on. As the wall of water rushed down stream it would wash away the houses on the right side of the creek as the creek bent to the left, and then take the houses on the left side further down when the next bend was to the right.

Remembering the Victims of the Buffalo Creek Disaster

Killed:

Brookie Mae Adkins, 31, Lundale, WV
Lonnie Lee Adkins, 7, Lundale, WV
Mary Jane Adkins, 5, Lundale, WV
David B. Adkins, Sr., 27, Lorado, WV
David B. Adkins, Jr., 4, Lorado, WV
Steven Albright, 17, Lorado, WV
Sylvia Albright, 39, Lorado, WV
Janice Bailey, 32, Saunders, WV
Kimberly K. Bailey, 6, Saunders, WV
Jason Bailey, Jr., 11, Saunders, WV
Rhoda Rene Bailey, 8, Saunders, WV
Carla J. Bailey, 18 months, Saunders, WV
James Bailey, Jr., 16, Amherstdale, WV
John H. Bailey, 58, Lundale, WV
Eleanor Bailey, 44, Lundale, WV
Milton Baker, 71, Lundale, WV
Effie Baker, 68, Lundale, WV
Joyce Bartram, 40, Lundale, WV
Betty Lee Black, 51, Lundale, WV
Edith Blankenship, 61, Lorado, WV
Rebecca Broady, 15, Lundale, WV
Donna Sue Browning, 21, Lundale, WV
Norman B. Browning, 3, Lundale, WV
James Brunty, 82, Kistler, WV
Dessie Butcher, 57, Lundale, WV
Leonard Butcher, 66, Lundale, WV
Ballard Carter, 36, Lundale, WV
Janice H. Carter, 29, Lundale, WV
Matthew Carter, 6, Lundale, WV
Lillian S. Carter, 3, Lundale, WV
Margaret L. Davis, 35, Stowe, WV
Mary Jane Davis, 8, Stowe, WV
Willie Dempsey, 42, Lorado, WV
Aletha V. Dempsey, 38, Lorado, WV
Berma Jo Dickerson, 20, Lundale, WV
Steven T. Dickerson, 18 months, Lundale, WV
James Dillon, 32, Lorado, WV
Thelma Dillon, 36, Lorado, WV
Curtis Dillon, 10, Lorado, WV
Sharon Dillon, 13, Lorado, WV
Darla Dillon, 5, Lorado, WV

Photo: Memorial marker at a church in Buffalo Creek, listing the victims and the missing persons of the Buffalo Creek disaster. Courtesy of Library of Congress, Coal River Folklife Project collection (AFC 1999/008), American Folklife Center. Photographer, Mary Hufford.

Howard Dillon, 8, Lorado, WV
Ruth Ann Elkins, 29, Lundale, WV
Judy Ferguson, 27, Lundale, WV
Connie S. Ferguson, 18 months, Lundale, WV
Martha E. Gunnells, 21, Robinette, WV
David Gunnells, 3, Robinette, WV
Jessie Gunnels, 1, Robinette, WV
Etta P. Hatfield, 60, Lundale, WV
Layton O. Hatfield, 50, Lundale, WV
Ruth B. Hatfield, 53, Lundale, WV
Steven Hatfield, 16, Lundale, WV
Albert O. Hedinger, 34, Godby, WV
Angela J. Hopson, 2, Crites, WV
Margaret Y. Jarrell, 42, Lundale, WV
Karen Jarrell, 16, Lundale, WV
Patrick Jarrell, 24, Lundale, WV
William L. Jarrell, 50, Lundale, WV
Lottie May Jarrell, 45, Lundale, WV
Andrew Johnston, 73, Crites, WV
Grace Kennedy, 71, Easley, SC (visiting relative)
Gary M. King, 24, Lundale, WV
Sharon A. Lester, 25, Saunders, WV
Denise Lester, 3, Saunders, WV
Norman Lester, 24, Saunders, WV
Dennatta Lester, 5 to 7, Saunders, WV
Opal Lester, 45, Saunders, WV
Barry K. Lester, 15, Saunders, WV
Rita J. Lester, 16, Saunders, WV
Mary B. Marcum, 44, Latrobe, WV
Diana L. McCoy, 18, Amherstdale, WV
Kimberly McCoy, 3, Amherstdale, WV
Jesse Messer, 35, Lorado, WV
Augusta Miller, 69, Pardee, WV
Robert Murray, 71, Lundale, WV
Wandell Osborne, Sr., 37, Lundale, WV
Jeanette Osborne, 35, Lundale, WV
Regina Osborne, 12, Lundale, WV
Carolyn Osborne, 20 months, Lundale, WV
Geneva Osborne, 11, Lundale, WV
Wandell Osborne, Jr., 15, Lundale, WV
Henrietta Owens, 22, Lundale, WV
Thomas Owens, 3, Lundale, WV
Herbert Peters, 71, Pardee, WV

Martha Peters, 71, Pardee, WV
Callis Perry, 81, Pardee, WV
Margie M. Prince, 42, Amherstdale, WV
Macie Queen, 54, Lorado, WV
Otis Ramey, 49, Latrobe, WV
Mattie Ramey, 45, Latrobe, WV
Virgie A. Ramey, no age give, Latrobe, WV
Marvel R. Scarberry, 73, Lundale, WV
Goldie Sipple, 38, about 38, Lorado, WV
Anita Smith, about 17, Lundale, WV
Florencio Sosa, 65, Lorado, WV
Mary M. Sosa, 46, Lorado, WV
Gladys Staton, 25, Lundale, WV
Kevin Staton, 1, Lundale, WV
Della Trent, 69, Saunders, WV
Johnny Trent, 32, Saunders, WV
Gene Trent, 26, Saunders, WV
Henry Trent, 49, Saunders, WV
Wanda Trent, 39, Saunders, WV
Betty Frances Vernatter, 4, Lorado, WV
Thomas Vernatter, 65, Latrobe, WV
Ethel B. Vernatter, 65, Latrobe, WV
Roby L. Waugh, 45, Lundale, WV
James L. Waugh, 11, Lundale, WV
Grady M. Waugh, 18, Lundale, WV
Donald Waugh, 20, Lundale, WV
Larry K. Wauch, 5, Lundale, WV
April E. White, 11, Lundale, WV
Dora Wiley, 60, Latrobe, WV
Richard Wiley, 78, Crites, WV
Frank Lee Workman, 69, Lorado, WV
Three unidentified babies

Missing
Dorinda L. Adkins, 3 months, Lorado, WV
Samuel Carter, 20 months, Lundale, WV
Roscoe Clay, 74, Lorado, WV
James N. Davis, 2, Stowe, WV
Nancy Hopson, 1, Crites, WV
Donald McCoy, Jr., 18 months, Amherstdale, WV
Kathy Waugh, 8 months, Lundale, WV

100 Years After: The Battle of Matewan

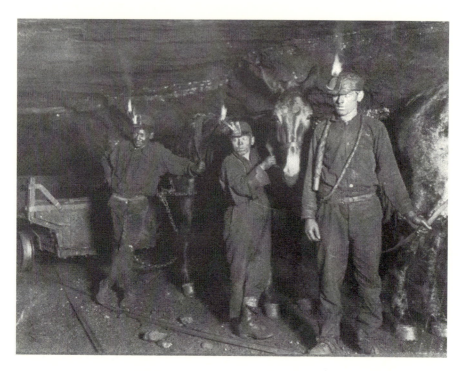

May 20, 2020, will mark the 100th anniversary of a battle that began an American civil war – a conflict of which most folks have never even heard, but one whose scars continue to mar the landscape of Appalachia even to this day.

Nearly fifty-five years to the day after General Robert E. Lee surrendered to General Ulysses S. Grant at Appomattox Court House in Virginia, laborers and lawmen 186 miles to the west in Matewan, West Virginia, took up arms to fight back against a new form of indentured servitude: Appalachian coal mining.

The story of what became known as the Battle of Matewan begins in the late 1800s, in the decades that followed the American Civil War.

Contrary to popular belief, much of what would become Southern West Virginia was actually fiercely loyal to the Old Dominion during the war; however, when the gunfire ceased, the redrawn map would now have them living in the newly created state of West Virginia.

For the most part, very little pushback ever came from the people regarding the changed political postwar landscape – wearied by war, most of the people of Southern West Virginia were simply grateful to see that terrible chapter closed and looked toward the future with eyes of hope.

Their land was rich in timber and new capital would soon be pouring into the area, offering jobs and railroads – allowing the timber on their land and the coal buried beneath their feet an avenue to get to distant markets.

In just a generation's time, many forgot their grievances toward the government in Wheeling and one by one the people of the mountains accepted the title, West Virginian. Eventually, the people of this state would become some of the most proud natives of any state in the entire nation.

Sadly, for many, the rich resources contained within their land proved to be a curse far more than a blessing.

As railroads became more common throughout Appalachia, armies of attorneys, land speculators and pure thieves were dispatched to the mountains in hopes of grabbing the rich resources of the land before the next financier was able to do so or before the people of the region realized the value of what they owned.

Photo: Dingess Tunnel, Used by permission from Norfolk Western Collection

Stories abound of how slick-tongued lawyers were able to deceive a largely uneducated populace into giving up their ancestral lands.

In a twist of sad fate, while the rest of the nation had ridden itself from the scars of slavery in the latter half of the 1800s, the once proud and free-spirited Appalachian people along the Tug Valley were becoming victims of the industrial revolution — the limitless resources buried deep beneath their homes proved to be an irresistible lust to many of the nation's wealthiest corporations.

The late Matewan resident, Joseph P. Garland, stated that his grandfather — who was illiterate — was tricked by corporate lawyers into giving up 1,666 acres of the family's land for a single shotgun.

Garland's story is not unique to Appalachia, at the turn of the century non-residents owned over half the land in Mingo County, West Virginia; as was the case in several other coalfield communities.

Observing this problem, William MacCorkle, West Virginia Governor and son of a Confederate major, warned the state legislature in his inaugural address on March 4, 1893, that "the state is rapidly passing under the control of large foreign and non-resident landowners." He cautioned that "the men who are today purchasing the immense acres of the most valuable lands in the state are not citizens and have only purchased in order that they may carry to their distant homes in the North the usufruct of the lands of West Virginia."

Sadly, MacCorkle, the sixth consecutive Democratic governor of West Virginia, witnessed his dire warning prove true.

Within a generation the coal barons had become so powerful in the region that they literally owned entire communities. Everyone, including the sheriff, school teachers, politicians and even local pastors, were on the payroll of the mine owners.

The miners themselves were viewed as an expendable commodity by the companies, who paid their employees in script (a form of private currency that could only be spent in company-owned stores). There the miners were forced to purchase essential goods at considerably marked up rates.

Miners who were not able to afford the high prices were offered credit, which indebted the miners even the more to the company.

Unthinkably, there were methods for miners to reduce their debt to the company store. In the book *Germinal*, it is written, "It was a known fact that when a miner wished to prolong his credit, he had only to send his daughter or his wife, plain or pretty, it mattered not, provided they were complaisant."

Giving no concern to the safety of their workers, early 20th century mines in West Virginia were among the most dangerous in the world. One historian has suggested that a U.S. soldier fighting in World War I stood a better statistical chance of surviving in battle than did a West Virginian working in a coal mine.

With limited pay and hardly any safety standards, miners throughout the Appalachian region began standing up against mine owners — forming unions and striking, demanding better working conditions.

Fresh off their victories in northern West Virginia and Pennsylvania,

United Mine Workers union organizers turned their attention toward the Southern West Virginia counties of Mingo and Logan.

The Mountain State's southern coalfields would prove a far more difficult task than union leaders expected, as entire law enforcement departments were on the payrolls of outside mining companies and strict policies were put in place forbidding unionization.

By May 1920, things in the Mingo County town of Matewan reached dangerously tense levels: Miners who lived in company owned houses launched a strike against their employer in hopes of gaining safer working conditions, getting paid in real cash and ultimately to be treated humanely.

Photo: Circa image of Matewan, West Virginia

Rather than comply with the miners' wishes, company owners instead reached out to the Baldwin—Felts Detective Agency.

Initially started in Southwest Virginia to serve as a private detective agency, Baldwin—Felts had moved into the more lucrative business of private security, working on behalf of mining companies to harass workers that did not fall in line.

Between 1913 and 1914, Baldwin–Felts agents were employed in squads to harass striking workers in Las Animas County, Colorado. They used an armored car with a mounted machine gun the miners called the "Death Special". The events culminated in the violent confrontation known as the Ludlow Massacre, when the Colorado National Guard used machine guns to kill 21 people, including miners' wives and children.

On Wednesday, May 19, 1920, a contingent of the Baldwin-Felts Detective Agency arrived on the No. 29 morning train to evict families that had been living at the Stone Mountain Coal Camp just on the outskirts of town.

The first family evicted was a woman and her children; the woman's husband was not home at the time. They forced them out at gunpoint and threw their belongings in the road under a light but steady rain. The miners who saw it were furious, and sent word to town.

The detectives carried out several additional evictions before eating dinner at the Urias Hotel and, upon finishing, they walked toward the train depot to catch the five o'clock train back to Bluefield, West Virginia.

While the detectives made their way to the train depot, they were intercepted by Matewan Chief of Police Sid Hatfield, a former miner and relative of Devil Anse Hatfield. Unlike so many other law enforcement chiefs of the region, Hatfield was a friend to miners and moved to push back against the company's hired guns – referred to as the miners as "thugs".

Claiming to have arrest warrants for detectives Albert Felts and his brother Lee Felts, Sid Hatfield ordered the men to surrender to their weapons and submit to his arrest.

Rather than comply, the Felts brothers pulled from their pockets their own arrest warrant for Sid Hatfield, ordering him to surrender his weapon and submit to arrest.

Matewan mayor Cabell Testerman inspected the detectives' so called warrant and is said to have exclaimed, "These warrants aren't worth the paper they're printed on."

Unbeknownst to the detectives, while the exchange was taking place, they had been surrounded by armed miners, many of whom had been evicted by the detectives earlier that day.

Watching from the windows, doorways, and roofs of the businesses that lined Mate Street the silence of the streets was soon interrupted by a barrage of bullets.

Who fired the first shot remains a hotly contested debate – even a century after the fact – but what was clear is that when the shooting finally ceased, two miners had been killed and the town's mayor, Cabell Testerman, lie dead on the streets.

On the other side, however, seven of the twelve Baldwin—Felts Detectives had been killed.

It is said that the shooting ceased just as the 5 o'clock train steamed into town as horrified passengers saw ten individuals dead around the train station and streets.

As the people of Matewan buried their mayor and mourned the loss of two of their miners, residents found solace in the fact that at least one local official had resisted bribes and remained faithful to the common-man. Sid Hatfield.

He became known as "Two-Gun Smile'n Sid Hatfield" and his fame grew throughout the mountains.

Sadly, Hatfield's fame would be short lived, as he and his deputy Ed Chambers were assassinated in neighboring McDowell County, West Virginia, on August 1, 1921.

Both men were unarmed at the time and were accompanied by their wives.

Several Baldwin-Felts agents shot them on the McDowell County Courthouse steps. Hit in the arm, and three or four times in the chest, Hatfield died instantly. Chambers was shot several more times, as his wife tried to defend him. He was finished off with a bullet in the head by Charles Everett Lively. None of the Baldwin-Felts detectives was ever convicted of Hatfield's assassination: they claimed they had acted "in self-defense."

Photo: *West Virginia lawman Sid Hatfield*

There was an outpouring of grief for the fallen local heroes at the funeral, which was attended by at least 3,000 people, and conducted with full honors from the Odd Fellows, Knights of Pythias and Redmen (he was a member of all of these organizations).

Six days following Hatfield's death, Mingo County coal miners rallied at the state's capitol building in Charleston, demanding the right to unionize.

Upon receiving news that their demands had been rejected, the miners became restless and began making plans to march back to Mingo County and revolt against their oppressors.

On August 24, 1921, an estimated 13,000 miners had gathered and began marching toward the mines in Mingo County.

"Impatient to get to the fighting, miners near St. Albans, in West Virginia's Kanawha County, commandeered a Chesapeake and Ohio freight train, renamed by the miners as the 'Blue Steel Special', to meet up with the advanced column of marchers at Danville in Boone County on their way to Bloody Mingo." But standing between the miners and the Mingo County mines they sought to capture was the West Virginia county of Logan and its fiercely anti-union sheriff Don Chafin.

Chafin was on the payroll of the Logan County Coal Operators Association and had assembled the nation's largest private armed force of nearly 2,000.

Taking the high ground, Chafin's men positioned themselves atop Blair Mountain, along the path of the miners' march.

By August 29th, the standoff had escalated into a full blown civil war between the mine-owned sheriff's office and the marching miners.

In an effort to avoid friendly-fire, all the miners agreed to wear handkerchiefs around their necks – red handkerchiefs.

"I remember Daddy leaving home to join the marching miners and he was wearing that red cloth around his neck," recounted one woman who was just a young girl at the time of the march. "The people who stood up to the mines were called rednecks."

Fearful that the same passions that had put an end to the +200 year old Russian government across the ocean less than four years earlier were being birthed in the hills of West Virginia, the White House was quick to respond.

On August 26, 1921, President Warren Harding threatened to send in federal troops and Army Martin MB-1 bombers to squelch the rebellion. After a long meeting in the town of Madison, the seat of Boone County, agreements were made convincing the miners to return home.

"However, the struggle was far from over. After spending days to assemble his private army, Chafin was not going to be denied his battle to end union attempts at organizing Logan County coal mines. Within hours of the Madison decision, rumors abounded that Sheriff Chafin's men had shot union sympathizers in the town of Sharples, West Virginia, just north of Blair Mountain—and that families had been caught in crossfire during the skirmishes. Infuriated, the miners turned back towards Blair Mountain, many traveling in other stolen and commandeered trains," writes one article.

In the days ahead, as many as 100 miners lost their lives in the uprising and nearly 1,000 men were arrested, charged with murder, conspiracy to commit murder, accessory to murder, and treason against the State of West Virginia.

Photo: UMW officials and members of the "miner's army" display a bomb dropped on them during the Battle of Blair Mountain.

With the conflict growing each day, President Harding made good on his promise, dispatching federal troops to squash the uprising.

Fiercely outgunned (most of the miners were armed only with hunting rifles and shotguns), union leaders called off the march and ordered the miners to return to their homes.

The immediate result of the battle was a decisive win for the mine companies and the United States government, as union membership in the coalfields of West Virginia plummeted – but the "rednecks" of West Virginia never gave up.

In 1935, more than a decade later, the miners of Mingo County finally tasted the fruits of their labor — winning the right to organize. Fortunately for the nation, they achieved this right without a communist revolution.

Interestingly, roughly fifty-years later, in the height of the Cold War, the people of Mingo County would again have their loyalties questioned following an incident that occurred in the Mingo community of Vulcan: With a rundown bridge which served as the only access to their secluded community nearly collapsed, the citizens of the town petitioned the US and West Virginia departments of transportation for repairs to be made – unfortunately, their requests fell upon deaf ears.

With the Cold War at its chilliest point, the people of this Mingo County community made an unprecedented move by writing to the Soviet Embassy in Washington, detailing their plight and requesting foreign aid from the communist super power.

Sensing an opportunity to shame the American government, the Kremlin immediately dispatched journalists to the United States and began showing signs that they would in deed help the forgotten West Virginia community.

Embarrassed by the attention their lack of assistance was receiving, state officials wasted no time in committing $1.3 million and began construction upon a new bridge for the tiny Mingo County community.

The Flying WV: How West Virginia's Most Iconic Symbol was Created

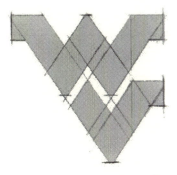

There is no symbol or logo that has held as prominent of a place in my home or heart as the famed "Flying WV".

As a child, it was synonymous with the football team my father taught me to cheer each autumn Saturday and thus it found its way onto the t-shirts and jackets my grandparents gifted me each Christmas.

Fast-forward a generation later and these two letters arranged diagonally have come to mean so much more than just that of a football team or university logo – for me personally, it has become a link to my childhood and one of the greatest identifiers of who I am as a man. On an even greater scale, however, the simple two-letter logo has surpassed the West Virginia State Flag as the premier symbol of the Mountain State.

Interestingly, this logo, which has become one of the most recognizable symbols in America, only dates back to the late-1970s. This begs the question, "How did this iconic logo get created?"

To answer this question, we reached out to *WVU Magazine* and they graciously provided permission to us to share a wonderful history they published in 2015 on this subject:

The Legend of the Flying WV
Written by Jake Stump & Illustrated by Chris Schwer
Courtesy of WVU Magazine

Sometimes It Takes Bad to Make Good:

After wrapping up six years with a winning record as Mountaineer head coach, Bobby Bowden left the helm in 1975 for a warmer climate at Florida State. There, he'd go on to establish a legendary 34-year career leading the Seminoles to two national championships.

With Bowden gone, so were the WVU victories. Following Bowden's departure, the Mountaineers slogged through four consecutive losing seasons (1976-79).

The Mountaineers could not even lose with style, so to speak, in those darkened days.

The distinct gold-and-blue color scheme and Flying WV logo we've come to adore did not exist at that point. Instead, football players bore a bronzesque gold helmet emblazoned with a blue outline of the state of West Virginia and the letters "WVU" inside an oval.

Blah.

The gold of the helmet did not reflect the gold utilized in our colors today. Think of a darker, Notre Dame-like gold, only uglier. The helmets also came in a white version.

By 1980, it was time for an extreme makeover: Mountaineer edition.

Leading this new revolution would be Don Nehlen, a former Bowling Green quarterback who later coached at his alma mater and served a two year stint as quarterbacks coach at the University of Michigan.

He was now charged with rebuilding the WVU football program.

When he arrived in Morgantown in December 1979, he dove headfirst into the game film.

But there was one glaring problem. He couldn't tell which team was WVU.

"I had trouble figuring out which team West Virginia was," Nehlen said. "The uniform was white. The helmet was white, and had the state of West Virginia on it. You really couldn't tell that unless you held one in your hand.

"I thought the colors were supposed to be blue and gold. I wanted a distinct helmet. I wanted everybody to know that when West Virginia University hit the field, they'd know who we were."

Nehlen shared his vision with the equipment manager, Mike Kerin. The coach was seeing dark blue and gold. After all, Nehlen had just come from Michigan, whose colors and logos bear a slight resemblance to WVU's.

He told Kerin, "I want a dark, blue helmet, and I want a WV on both sides."

The Confusion:

At this stage of the game, the story gets murky.

Nehlen claims he and Kerin sat down and drew designs for the new logo.

But no one else—Kerin included—recalls that ever happening. Kerin asserts that he and Nehlen never drew any sketches.

They were no van Gogh and Monet.

"I can't draw a stick man," Kerin readily admits. "I've had to diffuse some of the tales from over the years.

People come up to me and say, 'You developed the logo.' No, I didn't. I didn't design it." The concept around a football logo designated to stand out and unite did emanate from Nehlen, Kerin said.

This is how he remembers it: While they discussed the idea, putting it to paper would pose a greater challenge.

Kerin wound up at a sporting goods trade show in Chicago seeking ways to bring the new logo—whatever it would be—to life. There he met with a decal company and asked for ideas.

The company furnished a few designs. They were all duds.

Back in Morgantown, Kerin shared the company's sketches with Mike Parsons, then sports information director and now deputy director of athletics at WVU. None of the designs struck a fancy with any of the football officials.

From Parsons' end, he was scrambling to put together the 1980 football media guide. Before his office could print one, they needed the new logo.

"We couldn't use pictures from the '79 season on the cover of our publications because the uniforms were going to be different," Parsons said. "The media guide came out in the summertime. I thought, 'How do I handle the cover of the media guide? How can I depict the future?'"

Parsons, by the way, could not confirm Nehlen's version of the story, either.

The design had to come from someone or something, right?

Leave it to a Stranger to Come to Town and Solve the Problem:

While Nehlen, Kerin and Parsons can't agree on the particulars behind the design of the logo, they acknowledged the involvement of one man, and he hails from Kansas City.

John Boyd Martin grew up in the small Midwest town of Ottawa, Kansas, and had no real ties to WVU—other than the fact that his brother, Dick Martin, served as WVU's athletic director at the time.

A renowned portrait artist, graphic designer and illustrator, Martin had designed publication covers for multiple World Series, MLB All-Star games, and an NBA All-Star game. He'd done work for several professional sports teams including the Kansas City Chiefs, Atlanta Braves, and New York Mets.

Recruiting the artful talent of Martin was a no-brainer.

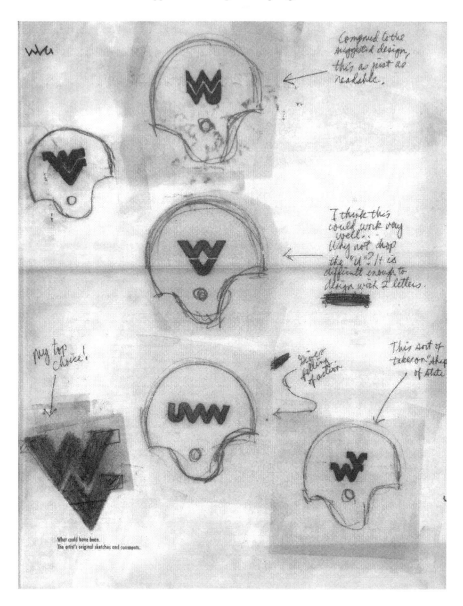

What could have been.
The artist's original sketches and comments.

Nehlen said that once he and Kerin drew a rough sketch of the Flying WV logo, they sent it to Martin to "clean it up."

Again, conflicting stories arise.

According to Kerin and Parsons, they sent Martin those "godawful" sketches drawn by the sports decal company.

"He (Martin) tells us, 'Those look like crap,'" Kerin said.

They asked Martin to produce his own sketches for the new logo. After a few days of scribbling with a pencil, Martin nailed it.

What we now know and love as the Flying WV was born on a sheet of wax paper.

Martin's main inspiration? Mountains. Yes. West Virginia has mountains. WVU's mascot is a mountaineer. Such an obvious fit.

"The first thing I did was play around with the initials," Martin said. "When you put a W and a V together, you had mountains. They may call it the Flying WV but to me, it depicts mountains."

As a graphic designer, Martin knew that successful corporations have "honest, simple" logos. Case in point: the Nike swoosh, the McDonald's arches, and the Apple apple.

The WVU logo would be simple. It would be a W and a V. Anything beyond that would've been overkill.

"You could've incorporated the 'U' in some way, but, to me, that would complicate it, especially for a helmet design," Martin said. "You could've added the face of a mountaineer. But that would just complicate it, also. A 'WV' is more adaptable and direct."

Mountaineer football officials knew they had a winner once they saw Martin's design.

"Everyone agreed it was distinctive and would be our new helmet decal," Kerin said. "We sent it back to Martin and told him we liked that one. Then he sent back a camera-ready negative and a bill for $200."

The emblem soon made its first appearance on the cover of the 1980 media guide. It was game time.

Flying WV: Prepare for Takeoff:
The date of September 6, 1980, marked many firsts for the WVU football program, and the University as a whole.

As WVU prepared to host the Cincinnati Bearcats in a season opener, it would be Coach Nehlen's first game leading the Mountaineers.

Not only did the game introduce a new coach, but a new stadium.

Beforehand, the original 38,000-seat Mountaineer Field had been situated on WVU's Downtown campus, around the current Life Sciences Building. Because of downtown expansion, officials decided to build a new, bigger stadium near the College of Law and Ruby Memorial Hospital. The "new" Mountaineer Field would cost $22 million and accommodate 50,000 fans.

That fall day also introduced the Flying WV and the football team's new helmets and uniforms to the masses.

The game remains one of the most memorable in Mountaineer history—not due to the game itself (WVU romped Cincinnati 41-27)—but because of the pageantry surrounding it.

To a thunderous applause, John Denver treated fans to a performance of *Take Me Home, Country Roads.*

Nehlen's Mountaineer coaching debut foreshadowed the upcoming years of his reign, which he believed played a part in the Flying WV's allure.

"Had we lost like crazy, maybe the logo wouldn't have caught on so much," Nehlen said.

Within a couple of years, the emblem appeared on hats, mugs, shirts, posters, among other items.

"That 'WV' became the link between the football team and our fan base," Nehlen said. "They all wanted it. Now it's on every daggone thing imaginable."

Sports Illustrated named it a top logo in college sports in one 1980s issue. In 2001, the magazine ranked the WVU football helmet sixth on a top 10 list of helmets.

No one fathomed that Martin's design would ultimately turn up in nationally televised events, on the heads of Hollywood celebrities and the backs of cars from coast to coast.

In 1980, brand recognition and corporate identity were not at the top of the University's list. Martin didn't see huge dollar signs in his design, either.

"As far as identity, it has become truly one of the greatest identifiable logos in the country," Martin said. "I didn't realize something like that would take off."

Martin visited Morgantown a few years after designing the logo and was floored by what he saw.

"The logo was everywhere," he said. "They took this thing and went crazy. Not only was it in the middle of the football field, but it was on newspaper bins. I went into a store and it was on everything. I even saw it in the grass in front of someone's house on their lawn."

Martin has encountered his design outside of West Virginia. Every time he sees someone donning the logo, he jokes that they "have great taste."

"I'm quite honored by it all," Martin said. "It's an awesome feeling knowing you were able to make that kind of contribution to an institution of that magnitude. Every time I watch a WVU game, I reflect back on something very special."

In its first year, 1980, the logo appeared only with the Mountaineer football team. Acknowledging the rising popularity of the Flying WV, other athletic teams began to adopt it in the following years.

Academics and administrators at the University, however, expressed lukewarm feelings toward the new emblem. Some complained the logo was missing the 'U' in 'WVU,' therefore, they argued that it did not fully represent the University.

But that stance would not last. WVU adopted it as the University's official logo in 1985. A WVU Alumni Magazine article that year read, "The Flying WV captured the fancy of West Virginians with amazing speed after it was introduced in 1980."

The story credited four consecutive bowl appearances to the emblem becoming a household fixture.

"If we turned out to be a lousy football team, I don't think the logo would be on any cars," Nehlen said.

No one predicted that a $200 investment for a helmet logo would ultimately turn into an internationally recognized symbol.

The Flying WV was first used on products in commerce in the same year of its birth. In 1980, products bearing the logo included electric lamps, decals, and T-shirts, said Marsha Malone, director of Trademark Licensing at WVU.

Today, the emblem is not only on just those products. It's on grave markers, toasters, fishing rods, golf carts, and waffle makers. There were even talks of making a Mountaineer Cola in the mid-1980s.

Some diehard Mountaineer fans have it tattooed on their skin.

Big-name celebrities such as Leonardo DiCaprio, Ben Affleck, Jennifer Garner, Brad Paisley and Randy Moss have been spotted in WVU gear.

Photo: Appalachian Magazine founder Jeremy Farley wearing a "Flying WV" hat.

The logo's presence may be widespread, but the heart and soul of the emblem remains embedded at WVU.

WVU is one of the top royalty producing colleges in the country thanks to the sale of officially licensed WVU gear—much of which includes the Flying WV.

Trademark royalties are used to assist with funding WVU athletic scholarships, cover the costs associated with administering the trademark licensing program, and to help fund other University marketing initiatives,

Malone said.

"The Flying WV contributes directly, in a financial way, to the wellbeing of the University through its use on licensed products," Malone added. "Of course, it also contributes in many other ways. It's a symbol of a state's pride in its school and a school's pride in its students and graduates.

"Seeing the Flying WV is like coming home."

WVU authorizes a large variety of products available in the marketplace. Through its licensing agent, the Collegiate Licensing Company, WVU has more than 500 licensees authorized to produce merchandise bearing WVU trademarks. Prominent companies include Nike, Perry Ellis, Tommy Hilfiger, Upper Deck, and Victoria's Secret.

All of this for $200.

That's the evolution of the logo, and as far as its innovators are concerned, it shall evolve no more.

"There have been three coaches since me (Rich Rodriguez, Bill Stewart, and Dana Holgorsen) and they've kept the logo and helmet," Nehlen said. "I told Rich when he took over, 'Don't mess with that helmet. That's the thing that sets us apart.'"

Old Time Mountain Religion: Foot Washings
Written by James Britton Cranfill in 1916

My father and mother were members of the Hardshell Baptist Church. It was made up of most excellent people. The Hardshell Baptists are very like the Missionary Baptists in their creed but differ somewhat in the interpretation of their creed.

On a certain Sunday, I went with my father and mother to the old time rawhide lumber church down on the south side of the Prairie. You may not know what rawhide lumber was, it was lumber sawed from oak trees. It was called rawhide lumber because it wouldn't stay put. It worked beautifully when green, but when the lumber dried under the heat of the summer sun it warped in every direction. This rawhide lumber warped in every conceivable fashion. For that reason, it had to be nailed very securely. If it were not thus nailed when green it never could be nailed because a nail can't be driven through a rawhide lumber plank after it seasons.

This church had a pine lumber floor and pine lumber seats many of which did not have any backs to them. On this particular Sunday Brother Abe Baker preached and then my father preached and Brother John Baker closed with an exhortation. These dear people would begin their services at about eleven o'clock in the morning and close them sometime in the afternoon, the time for the benediction varying with the number of preachers present and with the time it took for the Lord's Supper and the Foot Washing. After all three sermons had been duly preached and a closing hymn had been sung, Brother Baker came down out of the pulpit, opened his Bible and read the following verses from the 13th chapter of John: Now before the feast of the

"He riseth from supper, and laid aside his garments; and took a towel, and girded himself. After that he poureth water into a bason, and began to wash the disciples' feet, and to wipe them with the towel wherewith he was girded... Ye call me Master and Lord: and ye say well; for so I am. If I then, your Lord and Master, have washed your feet; ye also ought to wash one another's feet."

Preparation had been made by the deacons in anticipation of this exercise. The bread and wine had been procured as well as the basins and towels and water for the foot washers.

I reluctantly reveal a secret here. These dear good people when a foot washing time was approaching always very carefully washed their feet before they went to the foot washing. Not only that, but they put on the cleanest kind of clean hosiery. After Brother Baker had read the Scripture, I have quoted he laid aside his coat, girded himself with a towel, poured water into a basin and approaching Deacon Jack Bellamy, he knelt in front of him and said, "Brother Bellamy, may I wash your feet?"

Brother Bellamy assented and the dear man of God thus kneeling in front of Deacon Bellamy began to wash his feet.

Deacon Bellamy in the meantime had removed his shoes and stockings.

While this was going on the women of the church at the other end of the building were carrying on the same exercises. The men washed each other's feet and the women did likewise.

The greatest of decorum was preserved and the occasion was always a most solemn one. The foot washing began after the Lord's Supper was concluded. They first took the bread and wine just like other Christians do. This was done in great solemnity and then the foot washing followed.

After Brother Baker had washed Brother Bellamy's feet, Brother Bellamy, in turn, washed Brother Baker's feet. At the same time, my father was busy washing the feet of old Brother Asa Bellamy and he, in turn, washed my father's feet.

It was thus that going from one to the other and reciprocating this evidence of humility and love these dear people proceeded with their foot washing.

Many were the strangers who came down Hallmark's Prairie way to witness the foot washing exercises. But in every case as far as I can recall, those who came to scoff remained to pray.

There was nothing laughable in this solemn religious observance. Whatever else may be thought of it or said of it, it was true and will remain ever true that these simple folk believed profoundly that they were doing the will of God.

I must testify to be sincere that on every occasion when I was present at a foot washing, there was what the dear old folks would call "a splendid meeting."

They would when the exercises were concluded grasp each other's hand, shed tears of Christian joy, give voice to expressions of tenderest Christian love, and oft times these dear old soldiers of the Cross would be clasped in each other's arms.

Many were the misunderstandings and embryo feuds that would be settled on these foot washing occasions. No man could ever allow an enemy to kneel and wash his feet and no man could ever remain an enemy of the man whose feet he had washed. It was thus that whatever the meaning of the teaching of the Scriptures the ceremonial had its part in cementing the hearts of these dear people in the tenderest bonds of Christian and neighborly affection.

Now and then as the exercises would close some of the sisters would shout aloud for joy.

High School Student: Who Controls Our Fate?
Written by Rachel Musser
Highschool Junior

Many people believe that you are in control of your own destiny, but I disagree with this statement. I believe that our destiny has a lot to do with our actions, but I also believe that our destiny is in God's hands. The old man in *The Alchemist* said, "The world's greatest lie is that at a certain point in our lives, we lose control of what's happening to us and our lives become controlled by fate."

There is no certain time that we lose control of what is happening in our lives, but it is when we are born that our lives are taken out of our hands and put into One much greater than we could even describe. Our God has known our fate from the moment we began growing inside our mothers or even before that.

Some may say that One cannot hold the face of every single person in this world all to Himself, but His love for us is unconditional and everlasting. Sometimes journeys along the way may be rough to get through, but He has put that rough patch in your life to make you stronger and a better human. I have had many bad experiences that I feel like have lasted a lifetime, but I know that God put those hard times in my life for a reason. He is helping me to find my final destination. God does everything for a reason, even if it seems like the whole world is against you, just know God will always be right by your side.

Most people believe they can control their fate because they think they are always doing what is right for them. People think their fate is in their hands and nobody else's because it is their life and they can do what they want. A lot of the time what people think is best for them or what they think they want isn't really what is best for them. God always knows what He is doing with your life and He always will as long as you are faithful to Him, God is with you through the good times and the bad. Our fate cannot be determined by one's choice, but by our actions and our way of life.

God will lead you in the right direction as long as you follow Him. All you have to do is praise God and call upon Him. Our fate is whatever we make it out to be with God's help, guiding us in the right direction.

The Confusing Process of Determining Easter's Date Each Year

Appalachian Magazine

Most holidays are pretty easy to remember, we all know what happens on January 1, July 4 and December 25. These are easy holidays to remember as they're on the exact same date each year.

Other holidays and special days are a bit more confusing. Thanksgiving, for example, falls on the fourth Thursday of every November and election day is always on the first Tuesday after a Monday in November.

As wordy as the ingredients to determine which November morning is election day, however, it pales in comparison to the formula used to determine Easter.

To put it simply, the work required to determine which day of the year Easter falls on is anything but simple – in fact, it's quite complex. With this being said, it does always fall between the dates of March 22 and April 25.

How's Easter Determined?

In 325 AD, the *The First Council of Nicaea met* to establish rules regarding the holiday of Easter. The council established two rules for the holiday: 1.) Independence of the Jewish calendar and 2.) Worldwide uniformity.

No details for the computation were specified; these were worked out in practice, a process that took centuries and generated a number of controversies.

Today, the formula we use determine Easter is uniform and well established. Easter always occurs on the first Sunday after the first full moon that occurs after the vernal equinox (first day of spring). This full moon is referred to as the Paschal Full Moon.

Though wordy, this isn't all too difficult to determine in itself, unfortunately, there's a wrench that must be thrown into things to further complicate it: The church has decided to always consider March 21 as the first date of spring, even though the vernal equinox can occur as early as March 19 or as late as March 21.

Because of this decision, Easter always falls on the first Sunday after the first full moon after March 21.

Determining Easter 2020

Using March 21 as the first day of spring, the first full moon falls on Wednesday, April 8, which would then make Sunday, April 12, 2020, the date for this year's Easter.

Was Jesus Crucified on a Wednesday?

Written by Villiam Frederick, Nashville, Tennessee, in 1900

The belief that Jesus was crucified on a Wednesday and not a Friday, as popular tradition dictates, is widely held. One Presbyterian minister from a century ago lays out an interesting case

Who can solve the following problem based on Bible truths without proving Wednesday crucifixion or contradicting the Scripture? It is a known fact that the feast of unleavened bread which is called the *Passover* (Luke xxii 1) always came on the fifteenth day of the first month (Lev xxiii 6). This day was called the *Passover* from the fact that it was during the night of the fifteenth that the death angel smote all the first born of Egypt and passed over all Israel.

The day before the feast was called the preparation of the *Passover* because they killed the *Passover* on the fourteenth day of the first month (2 Chron xxxv 1) and prepared it to be eaten the following night. We know Jesus was crucified on the fourteenth because John says it was the preparation of the *Passover* when it occurred (John xix 14). We also know that Jesus was crucified on the fourteenth because it occurred the day before the *Passover* Sabbath which always came on the fifteenth no matter what day of the week it happened to come (Num xxviii 17-18). Jesus was buried as this Sabbath drew on.

It is also a known fact that Jesus came from Jericho to Bethany on Friday when he attended the last *Passover*. John says this occurred six days before the *Passover* (John xii 1). This shows that Friday came six days before the *Passover* the year Jesus was crucified.

The facts above give all the necessary elements of a clear and easy mathematical problem as follows: Jesus came from Jericho to Bethany on Friday six days before the *Passover* fifteenth and was crucified on the fourteenth.

What day of the month did he come to Bethany and what day of the week was he crucified? It is evident that if Jesus came to Bethany six days before the *Passover*, he came on the ninth because six from fifteen leaves nine. If the ninth was Friday then the fourteenth must have been Wednesday. This seems to prove that Jesus was crucified on Wednesday instead of Friday or that he did not come to Bethany six days before the *Passover* as John says. So far as the writer can see, there is no scriptural evidence for Friday crucifixion. The proof for Wednesday crucifixion is abundant in both the Old and New Testaments.

—Part Two—
Living the Good Life

"Spring Has Sprung"

—Part Two—
Living the Good Life

B&Bs, Trees, & Peas… Traveling Appalachia
Southwest Virginia's APEX Center is Becoming a Top Venue – Pg. 66
Five Day Bike Ridge Through Appalachia – Pg. 67

—Featured—
Blue Papa's Bible – Pg. 73

Profiles & Heartwarming Stories
A March to Remember – Pg. 77
The Meteorologist Turned Comedian – Pg. 80

Southwest Virginia's APEX Center is Becoming a Top Venue for Events & Shows

Wythe County's APEX Center (Appalachian Regional Exposition Center) has enjoyed a run of great events in recent weeks, ranging from bucking saddle broncs and jackpot barrel racing to high-flying monster trucks and a demolition derby that featured crazed cars crashing in an arena of mayhem .

In total, this year's events have sold more than 10,000 tickets and brought tens of thousands of dollars in additional revenue to the community.

The events are but a snapshot of the potential the 2,000 seat arena has to offer and as the facility enters its second full year of operation local officials are desiring to see the calendar expand.

Located at the crossroads of Interstates 77 and 81 at Exit 77, the APEX Center serves as Wythe County's largest indoor venue and has the capability to host a myriad of events, including trade shows, motorsports, concerts, and circuses, as well as athletic and agricultural events.

"We're pleased with the events we've had this year and are excited about many of the upcoming items on our schedule," said APEX Authority chairperson Cory Aker. Aker went on to say that many of the new Authority members have expressed their desire to focus on providing a better customer experience, as well as finding ways to reduce the operational cost of the arena.

This vision is shared by Wythe County Board of Supervisors chairman Brian Vaught, who stated, "This year, the board of supervisors made five new appointees to the APEX Authority. We are encouraged by what we're seeing but fully realize there's still a lot of work left to be accomplished. The taxpayers of Wythe County deserve for the facility to be well managed and accountable — we're pleased that the new Authority Board shares in this belief."

In the opening weeks of 2020, the APEX Center played host to a monster truck race, horse barrel racing, the Appalachian Indoor ShowDown Go Kart Race, Garden Brother Circus, Motocross as well as several other events.

Individuals interested in learning more about the APEX Center are encouraged to visit www.apexcenter.org or call 276-335-APEX.

"Spring Has Sprung"

Five Day Bike Ride Through Appalachia
Written by Charlie Myer in 2013

Charlie Myer is a retired project manager with a love for bicycling. In addition to cycling, Myer creates various pieces of furniture from discarded bicycle parts. Myer's bicycle travels can be followed on his blog, BackRoadsofIndiana.Blogspot.com

In mid-June a group of fourteen met in Grayson, Kentucky, for my 19th year of remote road rides in the Midwest. Riders from Mississippi, Indiana, Kentucky and one from Oregon returned for a dose of back country riding on the most remote paved roads I could find. Pitfalls for this year were services along the way. Lodging was not an issue, however, getting lunch daily became a challenge.

Day 1 – Grayson, Kentucky to Louisa, Kentucky:
We had intended to eat at Paw Paw's near Willard run by locals, however, a follow-up call earlier in the week found that [they] were only open on the weekends. Staff at the hotel in Grayson recommended Weavers Market / Bakery run by a Mennonite group.

This turned out to be great, allowing us to purchase deli sandwiches and wonderful homemade fig bars for a picnic along the route.

Speaking of the route, most attending the ride have dumbed down after a few years of attending and aren't interested in map reading, que sheets or GPX tracks. They return for some of the best road riding around; with narrow paved roads, very minimal traffic, and scenery that can knock your socks off.

So for me it's a piece of cake after wintertime research and a GPS.

This year started off with a little operator error in that I had not turned off the auto-reroute on the GPS. We had taken a diversion from the planned route to the bakery and the GPS then rerouted us on the shortest route to Louisa. All were cruising along while I was scratching my head thinking "why are we on KY 1 so long?"

Stopping the group a few miles further I fessed up that the leader had messed up and we were now heading out on uncharted roads to get back on the route. All were fine with maybe a little concern from two new members.

The rest of the first day went well with a stop for our deli sandwich at a beautiful family cemetery along the way. A couple of dogs joined us first then Harvey stopped over to see what was up. He lived behind the cemetery and took care of the family resting place. Harvey told us of his seven brothers only two remained. I asked him if he wanted a beer which got a quick "sure" and a trip to the cooler. He looked among the darker beers scratching his head then picked out a Sam Adams and smiled.

We traveled on in the back country and interesting road names arriving at the Louisa Best Western with 60 miles or so and ready for some cold brew. Dinner at a local Italian restaurant.

Day 2 – Louisa, Kentucky to Chief Logan State Park, West Virginia:

The group started out in Louisa, Kentucky, along the Tug Fork River then across the river into West Virginia.

Most river crossings are on highways but the chance to get on Tug River Rd. came quickly – a narrow paved road along the railroad and river, then on to Salt Petre Rd. and finally Mill Creek Rd. all of which were true backcountry. A quick stop in Dunlow due to threatening skies and a brief conversation with local James.

He talked of his mother catching the train there when she was a child. James talked about the book "Last Train to Dunlow," a definitive history of Wayne County, West Virginia, during the turbulent time following the Civil War and through the coming of the N & W Railroad – it includes history of the CCC Camps in Wayne County, history of the land speculators, train wrecks and collisions.

After leaving James at the Dunlow Station, we stopped for sandwiches at Copley's Deli, south of Missouri Branch then backtracked to 12 Pole Rd. which is a paved abandoned railroad bed, now a road.

There are places where new road has been added over the years, but we stayed on the railbed road as much as possible. At one point we ventured on along the railbed as it became smaller and smaller finally ending at a mobile home! It was a U-turn time to head back to the roadway, but before making it back the rains came and we found a shelter at a local church.

Moving on after the rain, our plan was to stop at the Cabwaylingo State Park for lunch at one of their shelters. We arrived and within a few minutes a horrendous storm blew through depositing a dead tree in front and back of our SAG, close one! The storm passed, but the skies looked threatening so six riders sagged on to the hotel while the rest followed along toward the end. The weather held and all arrived at Chief Logan State Park in the mid-afternoon. The state park lodge is located at the top of a good climb with great views of the surrounding mountain tops.

Day 3 – Chief Logan State Park to Matewan, West Virginia:

The day started out with a great downhill from the lodge only to head back up, cross the highway and back down into the back country. The route was again beautiful and remote following along the creek, however, too soon, the valley began to narrow and we were headed up. The hill on Smokehouse Fork-Harts Creek Rd turned to be a killer and quite possibly the worst hill most of us have ridden. Making it up requires good low gears, strong legs and determination.

A stop at the top to refresh then right back down only to climb again going to Dingess.

The Dingess Tunnel was to be a high point of the day and did turn out to be a scary experience. The unlit tunnel is 3,327 feet long, paved, one way and supposedly haunted.

Being on bicycles we had prepared for the tunnel by placing the SAG

in front of the group to keep oncoming traffic from coming at us. We also had headlights and flashing tail lights on each bike. Even with these precautions, we found the trip through the tunnel to be dangerous with water and some gravel in places.

Should we return to the area on a bicycle we'll SAG through the tunnel or flag down a local pickup truck and beg for a ride through the tunnel. As friendly as most locals were in West Virginia, the request would probably be honored.

After passing through the tunnel we veered off and on Old NW Railroad Bed Rd. and 12 Pole Creek Rd. passing Laurel Lake. It's worth the time to use 12 Pole Creek as much as possible. While there is minimal traffic on the main road and it is downhill most of the way to Lenore and lunch.

Cheech's Pizza is run by Bev and Robert Adkins and their menu fit the bill well. Robert was on his way to work, driving a coal truck, when I talked to him in the parking lot.

Bev was in the kitchen doing a great job of preparing our lunch. She had thought we were coming the next day, however, they did a great job of fueling our engines. After the rush, Bev joined us in the dining room with many stories of the area and people. She was a hoot!

Leaving Lenore the only way was on West Virginia highways and four miles of US-52.

We maintained single line with space between the riders for safety, but we found that traffic was fairly low on both highways.

At Delbarton we turned onto WV-65 to cross over the mountain heading to Matewan. There's a new road plus a closed road that is not maintained! As we rode toward Matewan we turned onto Chaffin St. and used the paved trail under the highway and railroad entering the town through an open gate in the floodwall.

We stopped there for pics and talked to a local.

He mentioned that a flood four years back went high enough that gates for the railroad required closing to keep the town from flooding.

Inside the protected town we arrived at the Historic Matewan House B&B run by Sharon Garland.

Sharon had many goodies including two cakes, drinks and other snacks. W`e were in heaven with her hospitality and facility. Five nice rooms in the main house and a bunkhouse in the back. Her breakfast was clearly the best on the trip! To prepare, serve and cleanup the breakfast, she had three others

helping out. In town we found several interesting characters, a bear of a dog and a bluegrass singer in the pizza place across the street.

I walked into the place and found her on a small stage playing a guitar and singing to an empty room.

After a few minutes, I headed back to the B&B to get an audience. Several joined in and enjoyed an hour of great music and bonding with a local artist. What fun!

Day 4 – Matewan, West Virginia to Jenny Wiley State Park, Kentucky:

We passed through Matewan, then across the Tug Fork River into Kentucky. Now we were in the land of the Hatfield and McCoy feud.

Several historical plaques and a nice museum in Matewan's old train depot are worth a visit.

We biked southwest out of town on secondary roads with great views of the valley and many interesting sights! On road 1056 we left the Tug Fork River valley on a seemingly endless climb to a spectacular view of the countryside.

We paralleled US-119 on Big Creek Rd. to Sidney, where fix'ns were available for a picnic lunch. Along the way we encountered a stray kitten and a few obstacles in the road.

Leaving Sidney we headed north for around five miles again on Big Creek Rd. This was Saturday when the coal trucks did not run from the two local mines which we passed on our way to Rockhouse Fork Rd.

At this point, we began a 25 mile route meandering through some fabulous country. Only periodic residences with immaculate gardens, well-kept simple homes, and seemingly endless rolling traffic free road. None of the group pushed the pace as we bathed  in the scenery heading to Jenny Wiley State Park. Arriving at the park the more energized boys hauled the cooler full of refreshments down steps to a patio overlooking scenic Dewey Lake. A comfortable stay at the lodge refreshed the group for the last day into Grayson.

Day 5 – Jenny Wiley State Park, Kentucky to Grayson, Kentucky:

Leaving the lodge, we rode along Dewey Lake for eight miles then crossing the dam on our way to Paintsville for a stop at the IGA for lunch fix'ns!

The IGA wasn't open so we sent the SAG vehicle on past the town to find food. The peloton charged on with great scenery, couple of stiff climbs and interesting Kentucky roads with no traffic. The SAG van caught up with us near an abandoned strip mine where we refreshed with cool drinks.

On to Boone where the, closed on Sunday, grocery made another convenient place to regroup.

We then pedaled on, looking for a nice lunch stop and around the corner was the Cherokee Baptist Church which had just wrapped Sunday morning service. The pastor talked with several of the group and offered coffee and restroom facilities to the group.

After lunch, and around the 45 mile mark, the route slowly straightened and flattened, and suddenly a paceline was formed with the speed nearly doubling the last four days rate. It was going home time and they wanted to get there. It was a good feeling to know that everyone experienced a great ride through Appalachia.

"Spring Has Sprung"

Blue Papa's Bible
Remembering James Alfred Fitzgerald

Born in the mountains of Central Virginia just months after the stock market collapse of 1929, James Fitzgerald was the son of a World War I veteran and came to age during some of the most dark and turbulent days in world history.

He once reminisced to me that as a young boy, maybe about twelve or thirteen years old, he would rush through his chores and then race across the mountains to an overlook where he would spy young soldiers training prior to being deployed to Europe during the Second World War.

This was the world in which he grew up. An unincorporated community bisected by a now defunct railroad was his home. The Appalachian way of life was every bit as much a part of who he was as was the blue work shirts he wore on nearly every occasion.

When he got older, he would marry a girl 364 days his elder, a young woman named Virginia Marie.

To better provide an honest living for his family, they left the mountains of Nelson County, Virginia, and moved to the nearby big city of Lynchburg, where he would go to work in a place he always simply called "the foundry". In the decades that followed, he and Virginia would purchase a home, raise a son and a daughter together, and become a staple of their new neighborhood and church.

Unfortunately for me, it was not until he was 77-years-old that I first met him. I was in town to visit his granddaughter, a redhead that had captured my heart and one whom I would eventually capture her hand in marriage. Back in those early days, I don't recall interacting with the old man very much, but as I do remember, his accent stood out to me "like a sore thumb".

He spoke in a dialect linguists refer to as "Virginia Piedmont", a style common for his region of the Commonwealth. Statements like "four dogs" sounded like "fo-uh dahawgs", while words like "car" were pronounced without the r sound and "afraid" sounded like "uh Fred", though he very rarely ever spoke of being afraid of anything.

The days that followed our first meeting would be some of his most glorious and lonely, as in 2008 my wife and I would announce to him that he would again be a great-grandfather – hard of hearing, he was too busy educating me on why Rhode Island Reds were a better breed of chicken than Plymouth Rock chickens to comprehend what my wife was saying.

"We're having a baby," she screamed at him, smiling from ear to ear.

"Who's having a baby?" he responded.

"I am," she answered, to which his only reply was to break out into laughter, a jolly sound that was contagious, "heeeee, heeeee, heeeee…"

In short order, we would again find ourselves screaming into his ear that yet another baby would be present in our lives, but not before he lost his bridge of many decades – Virginia Marie died while working in a garden on one sweltering summer's afternoon.

I will never forget seeing him at the funeral.

In his typical fashion, he bragged to me about how he was able to bring the funeral home down on the price of his wife's casket. He then stood from his chair and turned to face the audience, "Marie knew exactly where she was going and I know exactly where she is right now. Ain't none of us know how much longer we have left, but I'm ready to see her today. If you're not ready, you better get ready!"

The new baby would be born just a handful of months after his wife's passing – quickly, days would turn to weeks, weeks to months and months to years and that baby, as well as her older sister, would grow into a duo of adolescent girls who would adore his every move.

Observing that his typical apparel was the blue work shirts commonly worn by hardworking men of his generation, the great-granddaughters would begin calling him "Blue Papa", convinced he wore blue because it was his favorite color -- at every chance possible, they'd insist on buying him all things blue in color.

While my daughters grew to adore him, I found myself admiring him the more with each passing day. His wisdom of mountain life, stories of

"Spring Has Sprung"

old and commitment to family and life, even after his soulmate was gone, were all attributes I envied. In short, he seemed like one of those people who would be around forever, a Rock of Gibraltar, a North Star.

After multiple miscarriages following the birth of our second daughter, my wife and I were finally blessed to see our third and final baby born, another girl.

In an effort to honor him, as much as her, my wife and I agreed that there would be no question as to the new baby's name, Virginia Marie. A man of few words and one who safeguarded his emotions, he was brought to tears when we told him the newborn infant's name.

He loved her and she loved him.

Growing older with each passing day, our family knew "the day" would eventually happen, but the 89-year-old Appalachian man showed no signs of slowing. Driving his new white van around town, polishing his red pickup truck, dragging around ladders to clean the gutters of his home, carrying downed branches from trees on his property – he worked 'til his final day on earth.

Hours away from Lynchburg, our family concluded a wonderful church service the Sunday before Christmas. The decorations were festive, the mood was jolly and life was excellent. Unfortunately, all of this was lost with a single phone call.

"Blue Papa" was gone.

In the weeks that followed, the family would begin the unenviable process of sorting through the man's earthly belongings. The first item they came to was his Bible. It was in the precise shape you would have expected from a man who lived the way he did – tattered, marked up and well-worn.

He was never a wealthy man —he was born a poor Appalachian Mountain child who just so happened to know the God of Heaven. He was a man of faith and faithfulness; however, one thing that everyone in the family has been able to appreciate was that his Bible was more than a coffee table decoration, it was the Book that dominated his life.

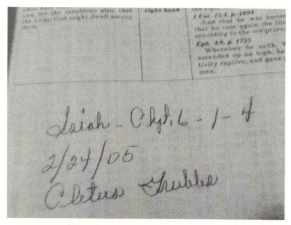

Nearly every page of that Old Bible was marked with sermon notes, verses circled or the name of a preacher who had spoke from that particular text.

Each handwritten note in the margins and each tattered page is a living example of the faith of a man who saturated his family in prayer and Scriptures.

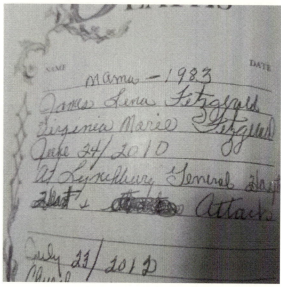

The man who lived thrifty and saved his entire life, leaving his children a paid for house and two vehicles left the entire world the greatest inheritance of all: An undeniable faith, evidenced by the condition of the Book he left behind.

A March to Remember:
Upon Returning Home, US Soldiers March to Grave of Fallen Friend

Republished by permission from Air Force News Service
Written by Airman 1st Class Zachary Vucic
Photos courtesy of U.S. Air Force Senior Airman Lauren Main

The morning of Aug. 8, 2012, Heather Gray was preparing an anniversary care package for her deployed husband, a tactical air control party member assigned to the 13th Air Support Operational Squadron at Fort Carson, Colo.

Around 8 a.m., a vehicle pulled into her driveway. She wasn't familiar with the vehicle and her children were asleep, so she decided not to answer the initial ringing of her doorbell. As the ringing persisted, her children awoke and prompted her to answer.

Heather opened the door to a colonel wearing his dress blues. Initially, she said, she just thought "It's (blues) Monday." Then, she noticed a chaplain standing, visibly shaking and clutching a piece of paper.

When Heather saw the pair, she recognized them as a casualty notification team. As a key spouse, she thought she had been chosen to go with them to deliver devastating news to another TACP family.

"The first words out of my mouth were, 'Oh no, who was it?'" she said. "(The colonel) said 'No Heather – it's David,' and it was like the whole world just went into tunnel vision. I had just talked to him six hours before that ... I just kept saying 'Are you sure it's David?' It was a very long process of putting it together ... that he was going to be the one who wasn't coming back."

Heather's husband, Maj. Walter David Gray, an Air Liaison officer assigned to the 13th Air Support Operations Squadron, was killed that day by a suicide bomber in Kunar province, Afghanistan.

Gray was hit by the second of two suicide bombers. After the first blast, he and his team rushed the scene to help when the second blast went off.

In his memory, 13 members of the 13th ASOS took on a 140-mile ruck march from Dover Air Force Base, Del., to Arlington National Cemetery, Va., arriving on the anniversary of David's passing.

"He made the ultimate sacrifice," said Master Sgt. Mitchell Polu, the NCO in charge of the 13th ASOS Delta Flight. "What we're doing right

now is nothing compared to what Major Gray, Heather Gray and his family and kids had to go through."

The TACP Airmen chose their route to provide much needed closure for the Airmen, Polu said. With four months left on their deployment, Gray's Airmen were unable to return from the war zone to escort him home or attend his funeral. Their grueling trek from the mortuary at Dover AFB to Arlington traced Gray's route to his final resting place.

For their visit, instead of driving or flying to Arlington, the ruck march was unanimously voted to be the most fitting way to honor their fallen brother.

"It meant a lot more for us to walk it ... this is (the TACP) way of doing things," said Senior Airman Justin Jackson, a TACP assigned to the 13th ASOS.

The Airmen of the 13th ASOS share one common sentiment toward

Gray -- he was like a father to them. He was the first one through the door and the last to leave. Polu said Gray spent one-on-one time with each and every Airman under his command.

"He cared so much about us," said Senior Airman Matthew Swift, a TACP assigned to the 13th ASOS. "I had two family members pass away while I was deployed, and when my gran'daddy passed ... he flew all the way to my (forward operating base) and spent the whole day there with me. He stopped what he was doing and came out just to see me."

That care and loyalty is now repaid by the TACP community to Gray's family. Every week, Heather said, members of the TACP community check up on her, to see if there is anything she needs, from moving furniture to child care.

"David always told me, 'If anything ever happens to me, my guys will take care of you,'" Heather said. "(The support) has been amazing."

Heather said it's not just the Airmen from the 13th ASOS, but the entire TACP community.

Gray's journey to the TACP career field started early in his career, when he completed TACP training as a young enlisted Airman. He later commissioned, and waited patiently for the career field to open to officers. Heather said the day it opened, Gray came home with a big smile on his face.

TACPs primarily act as a vital link between ground forces and the aircraft that support them. They put themselves in harm's way to ensure bombs are on target. Gray's choice to rejoin the career field and participate in the rigorous training again at age 37 was "a hard sell" to his wife she said.

"He just kept saying 'You don't understand, it's so different; it's what I'm meant to do,'" Heather said. (He said) "This is why I joined the Air Force.'"

The crew's journey to honor Gray was made possible through a combination of permissive TDY from their commander, donations from the TACP Association and the public, and out-of-pocket expenses in the form of both money and ordinary leave.

"To be with (his fellow Airmen) is very special," Heather said. "I don't really have words to describe how much it means to me that they're doing this. I love each and every one of them, and they truly are like having a family of older brothers. I'm very humbled and inspired by these guys, and I know that it's a direct reflection of what kind of leader he was for them."

Gray was posthumously awarded the Bronze Star with Valor, and his sacrifice inspired Heather to start a foundation and scholarship in his honor. Heather joined the Airmen for the last leg of the journey, with all three Gray children making the final mile. She said when things get tough, she hears her husband's voice reciting what has become a motto for her – "Finish strong."

Kristina Montuori: Former Meteorologist Finds Comedy to Overcome Life's Storms

In the mid-1990s, WDBJ-7 meteorologist Patrick Evans stopped by Fishburn Park Elementary School in Roanoke, Virginia, and introduced a group of third graders to the life of a meteorologist.

Seated in the public-school classroom was a self-described "awkwardly shy" eight-year-old girl who found Evans' talk about the science of weather to be nothing short of fascinating.

"Everything he talked about just sounded really cool and from that moment on I wanted to study meteorology."

This young girl's name was Kristina Montuori and in the

handful of years that followed, she would establish a name for herself in high school athletics as being one of the region's most gifted athletes.

Following high school, she received a scholarship to play NCAA Division I soccer at the University of North Carolina—Asheville where she became captain of her team.

The Southwest Virginia native would go on to fulfill her dream in 2010, graduating at the top of her class with a meteorology degree.

Shortly thereafter, Montuori moved to Tornado Alley for her first job at KTBS 3 in Shreveport, Louisiana.

It seemed everything was on track but after only four months on air, Kristina's seemingly healthy 48-year-old father suffered a fatal heart attack that turned her world upside down.

Her father's death dealt a devastating blow to the family and forever altered her life. She decided to return home to help her family, unfortunately, there were no TV meteorology job openings in Roanoke at the time.

The only media opening the former weather forecaster could find was at WSLS 10 as a producer, so she learned to produce newscasts and worked behind the scenes for a year before viewers in her hometown ever saw her on air.

"It was the darkest time of my life. I lost my father who was my best friend. I lost my dream career and I was working third shift doing something I hated. I was miserable but something inside me told me I was in the right place and that I had to keep going."

One morning, as Kristina was making her way out the door after an 11 hour shift, the chief meteorologist called out because his wife had gone into labor. The morning meteorologist was on his way home and the weekend person was out of town. The news room was in a state of panic as there were no meteorologists for the upcoming broadcast.

"I can do it," Kristina announced to a flustered newsroom.

"I am a meteorologist."

Though the news team was reluctant to put a third-shift producer on air, they had no other choice but to mic her up and hope for the best.

"I was exhausted and out of practice, but I knew I had to do it. The universe gave me a shot. I couldn't let it slip," she recalled.

"After the show I cried. It was a long, hard ugly cry… a happy one though. It was a release of all the pain I'd endured to get to that amazing moment. I rocked that show and I was proud of myself."

That successful show earned Kristina a part-time spot on the weather team which eventually turned into a fulltime position.

Despite her on-air, on-the-field and academic excellence, off camera, off the field and out of the classroom she struggled with self-confidence.

"People assume I'm a naturally confident person, but I'm really not. Growing up, I was painfully shy. Confidence is something I have to work at each day – even now. I have to work really hard and remind myself to think positively," she told Appalachian Magazine in a recent interview.

Though she may have been fighting these feelings internally, Southwest Virginia viewers never saw this side of the attractive and seemingly naturally confident meteorologist. Her charm, accurate forecasts and friendly demeanor propelled her to the status of local celebrity and she was named by *The Roanoker* as "TV Weather Person You Rely on Most".

Montuori says she owes a lot of her success to being a student of self-confidence, public speaking and "power posing," the belief that one's posture has a physical effect upon their hormonal and behavioral health; studying the theories and science behind confidence, body presentation and subtle communications nuances which separate passive people from individuals who possess a commanding presence.

"When I walked into rooms, I was constantly having to remind myself of everything I had read, 'shoulders back, stand straight, make eye contact, speak clearly…' At first this was awkward and robotic, but it eventually became effortless."

Despite her struggles with confidence, Montuori learned to adapt and grow into the person she wanted to be, even though it wasn't natural for her. "I became the funny person in my social circle and enjoyed being around people."

Each morning, viewers awoke to the smiling face of the well-figured blonde whose looks were surpassed only by her understanding of the complex science of weather; however, beneath the façade of fake hair-extensions and trained media voice was a weary woman who was suffering greatly from exhaustion and the stresses that accompany hometown stardom.

"I was waking up at 2:30 each morning because I was doing a morning show and not getting home until 1:30 or later in the afternoon – it's hard to have much of a life when your bedtime is 6 p.m.," she said.

"Whenever I'd go to the store, people I didn't even know would run up to me and give me a hug and I'd have to be the energetic person they knew on television and it was tiring – don't get me wrong – I loved the people and was touched that they felt comfortable with me, but it was also very hard to have a normal life."

"In the beginning, when I was new to the life of T.V. weather forecasting, I was driven by adrenaline and enjoyed every aspect of the job, but seven years into it, I was drained," she said, adding, "Most people have no idea how much work their television news crews put in — a lot of hours go into every half-hour broadcast."

In an extreme move of self-preservation, Montuori did something she never could have imagined only a handful of years earlier: She resigned from what had been her dream job.

With no children and very little holding her down, the meteorologist who also served as a morning show cohost realized she was in a position in her life where she could take advantage of the freedom her lifestyle afforded.

"I left WSLS 10 just to pursue happiness. I loved working there and my coworkers were great, but the news industry in general was just draining; the early mornings, late-night fundraising events, having to be 'on' anytime I walked outside had just become too much."

In addition to being emotionally drained, the Roanoke native said that she had also grown bored with the job, stating that she "just didn't feel challenged anymore."

Four months after leaving WSLS, while in Denver with some friends, the former television meteorologist did something that would have been unthinkable years earlier: She signed up for open mic at a comedy club and tried her hand at being a standup comedian.

"I thought I was going to be hilarious, but it turned out to be terrible. I learned really quick that there is a huge difference between conversational humor and stand up humor," Montuori laughed.

Despite falling on her face in the Mile-High City, the Southwest Virginia woman loved the rush and surge of adrenaline that accompanied being on stage and attempting to make people laugh.

Always a student, she began studying comedy and soon grew toward perfecting a style uniquely her own.

Initially performing in the Roanoke area, as Montuori's skills as a comedian developed, she soon realized that despite her love for the region, the opportunities as a comedian in Southwest Virginia were limited.

Kristina now travels wherever she can perform, but spends most of her time in Naples, Florida.

"My mother lives in Florida, the weather is warm and there are simply more opportunities for a new comedian," she said.

She has performed at The Orlando Improv and Off the Hook in Naples, Florida, and is building a portfolio opening for larger names.

"Breaking into the comedy scene is hard and time consuming. I'm still a student of comedy, but I feel like I'm getting better each time. My life is finally in a good place where I'm happy. I'm not worried about getting rich and famous. I earn enough money to pay for my needs and I'm just enjoying life," she said.

When asked about her plans for the future, the former Appalachian meteorologist was quick to interrupt by saying, "I always hesitate to say where my future is heading. I would love to have a talk show one day or get into acting, but I'm not thinking that far down the road. As long as I can keep enjoying what I'm doing I'll be happy. At this point, I wouldn't say I have a specific goal I'm working toward, I'm just trying to be the best me each day — It's a nice place to finally be."

—Part Three—
Straight Outta The 'Holler'

—Part Three—
Straight Outta The 'Holler'

Appalachian Living, Healing, Growing & Eat'n
Ancient Wisdom for Predicting the Weather – Pg. 86
A Generation That's Never Tasted a Real Tomato – Pg. 90
The Work to Restore Bobwhite Quail in Appalachia – Pg. 92
Coming 2024: Total Solar Eclipse – Pg. 96

—Featured—
Managing Snakes in a Residence,
Business or Other Occupied Space– Pg. 98

Tall Tales & Mountain Legends
Granny Myers' Curse – Pg. 103
The Crucifixion Legend of the Dogwood Tree – Pg. 106

Ancient Wisdom for Predicting the Weather

Excerpts from the 1738 book, "A Rational Account of the Weather, Showing Signs of its Several Changes and Alterations, Together with the Philosophical Reasons of Them"

Signs of Weather from Animals:

Birds – Creatures that live in the Open Air must needs be supposed to have quicker Sense of it than Men that live more within Doors, especially BIRDS that live in the Air that is Purest and Clearest and are apter by their Voices and Flights and other Motions to discover their Sensations of it Therefore those that have applied themselves to the Observation of the Signs and Prognostications of Good or Bad Weather have laid down these following Rules:

<u>Waterfowls</u>: Such as seagulls, moorhens, etc. when they flock and fly together from the Sea towards the shores, foretell Rain and Wind.

<u>Landbirds</u>: And contrariwise Land Birds as Crows, Swallows, etc. when they fly from the Land to the Waters and beat the Waters with their Wings do likewise foretell Rain and Wind.

Beasts – There are several sorts of BEASTS likewise that foretell rain. When sheep leap mightily and frisk about and push at one another with their heads. When Deer fight. When Asses bray or shake their Ears and are much annoy'd with flies. When foxes bark and wolves howl mightily.

When cattle leave off feeding and hasten to shelter under hedges and bushes. When cats rub their heads with their forepaws, especially that part of their heads above their ears and lick their bodies with their tongues, the reason of which is the humidity of the air incommoding their bodies by clogging their hair and obstructing their pores. The very same Reason may be given for Asses braying foxes barking and wolves howling.

Beasts do generally take delight in a wet air and it makes them eat their meat the better because the humidity of the air helps to relax the fibers of the stomach and open the glandules which transmit an acid juice that creates an appetite. Hence it is that sheep will raise themselves betimes in the morning to feed against rain and cattle and deer and rabbits will feed hard before rain; only heifers and oxen will put up their Noses and snuff in the air against rain.

Fishes – Fishes in the Sea or in Rivers do often predict rain by their playing towards the top of the water. The reason of which is this: Fishes love to keep from the air as much as they can when it is dry and swim lower and will not approach the air till it is moist.

Insects – Insects also and reptiles foretell rain. Earthworms will creep out of the ground and moles will cast up more earth and fleas bite more against rain and spiders creep abroad and flies are very troublesome, often dashing against a man's face. Bees do not stir or at least not far from their hives, ants quit their labour and hide themselves in the ground. For these Provident insects by a secret instinct of Nature find the air changed into moistness and clogged with vapours carry their eggs to a place of drier security.

Frogs will croak in ditches more than usually against rain.

Hornets likewise and wasps are foretellers of the weather. If they are seen flying together in greater numbers than ordinary in an evening, they foretell warm and fair weather the next day. But if in a dark and dull Day they are observed to betake themselves to their nests more frequently for shelter, you may then expect either rain, wind, or storms the next day.

Men – Even in men, aches, wounds, and corns are more troublesome either towards rain or towards frost. For the one makes the humours of the body to abound more and the other makes them sharper.

Signs of Weather from Solid Bodies:

Stones – Stones, especially marble, when they sweat or rather seem to sweat and boxes and doors, especially deal and pegs of wood when they draw and wind hard, are signs of wet weather.

The hardest and most solid wood will swell by the moisture of the air as appears by the difficulty of shutting our doors and windows in wet weather.

If a Pair of scales continues in equilibrium when loaded with two equal Weights one of which is of a more voluminous substance than the other as cotton or any body of a lesser specific gravity, the balance will depart from its equilibrium and incline to that more voluminous weight when the air is condensed with vapours: For the watery particles with which the air is loaded, will insinuate themselves more readily into this, than into the other weight, which being less voluminous.

Signs of Weather from the Heavens:

Sun – If the sun at his risings looks red and broader than usual, then many moist vapours are gathering. And if this happen in hot weather viz summer or autumn, violent showers of rain will fall, but not of long continuance, but if in winter or spring, settled rains but more moderate.

When the sun rises hollow -- that is somewhat obscured by clouds or hid in the cavity of a cloud – it foretells rain. When the clouds look reddish before the sun rising, it foretells wind. But if there be a mixture of black clouds with the red, it foretells rain.

Moon – The moon likewise has its signs. Thus a pale moon is the forerunner of rain. Red of wind. Clear of fine weather.

When the moon is compassed about with a very large circle or is dim and misty, then wind or rain follows or snow speedily or likely within twenty-four hours.

Two or three discontinued and speckled circles or rings round about the moon, foretell a great storm.

What I shall further observe concerning the moon is this… the full moon in April always brings rain, and that the new and full moon in August do the like. This rule has not failed above once in almost thirty times.

Stars – Nor are the stars (though at so great a distance) destitute of their signs. The stars seeming bigger than usually; pale, dull, and not twinkling shew the air is condensing to rain which will soon fall.

Also the stars appearing more bright and blazing than ordinary in Summer, is a sign of great winds and rain.

Likewise many stars appearing in the night and seeming a greater number than usual, and the wind at east in Summer, foretells sudden rain.

Clouds – If small clouds grow bigger and bigger in an hour or two, they signify a great deal of rain. On the contrary, if great clouds separate, waste off, and grow smaller and smaller, they signify fair weather.

White clouds in the summer time are a sign of hail, but in winter time they are a sign of snow -- especially when we perceive the air to be a little warm occasioned by some warm eruptions out of the clouds.

Rainbows – If after a long drought, the rainbow appears, it signifies rain: but if it appears after a long time of wet, it signifies fair weather.
A Rainbow in the Morning, A Shepherd's Warning;
A Rainbow at Night, A Shepherd's Delight.

If two rainbows appear together, it denotes fair weather for the present and rain two or three days after.

Signs for the Seasons:
It is an observation among country people that those years in which we have store of heps and haws do commonly portend cold winters and they ascribe it to Providence that reaches to the preservation of birds in such seasons.

Some people make their observations from nut trees. If in the year, they flower much, it foretells a plentiful harvest, sickly autumn and cold winter.

If the summer be dry and the wind northerly, but the autumn rainy and the wind southerly, then violent pains in the head, coughs, hoarsness and rheums, and to some consumptions are to be in the winter.

A Generation That's Never Tasted a Real Tomato

Photo: *Commercial tomatoes for sell, courtesy of InterestingPics*

It is undeniable that the tomato has become a staple food in the Western World, as American, Italian, Spanish, and Mexican diets are largely based upon this easily preserved fruit. A fruit the Supreme Court ruled to be a vegetable in 1893 in a case that challenged US tariff laws imposing a duty tax on imported vegetables but not fruits.

Regardless of what you call it, for generations millions of American children grew up anxiously awaiting the ripening of the year's first tomatoes as it signaled a near daily treat until well past the first frost.

Big, soft, juicy and sweet, America's tomatoes of yesteryear were culinary delights that were as beloved as any candy.

Whether sliced and heavily salted, slapped betwixt two pieces of bread with mayonnaise, or eaten raw, these tomatoes were nothing short of pure ecstasy and children craved these garden treats!

Fast-forward a handful of generations and American school children are throwing away tomatoes faster than the lunchroom cafeteria workers can slap them onto a tray.

What happened? Why have America's youngest fallen out of love with what was once its beloved fruit?

The answer may not surprise you all that much: It's not that our children have changed, it's that tomatoes have changed.

Tomatoes were once a seasonal treat enjoyed fresh out of the garden, but advances in science has made it possible for Americans to eat a red tomato year-round, anywhere in the nation.

The tradeoff, however, is that the scientifically modified plant simply isn't as good as it was a half-century ago.

In the 1950s, tomato breeders discovered a mutant phenotype which caused a tomato plant to ripen uniformly red, rather than retain a green ring around the stem as was previously the case.

After additional cross-breeding and modifying, scientists had created what seemed to be the perfect commercial tomato: One that was brilliantly red, would not spoil as quickly, was resistant to pests, and a plant whose skin was tough enough to not split or burst during thousands of miles of transport.

Unfortunately, for all of its selling points, the new tomatoes simply were not as tasty.

Old styles of tomatoes produced more sugar during the ripening process, which resulted in a sweeter and more flavorful fruit.

Today's more altered plants taste more like wet Styrofoam than the garden treat you may remember as a child.

The greatest antidote to saving another generation from despising tomatoes is by actually letting them taste what real tomatoes taste like: Heirloom Tomatoes.

Heirloom tomatoes are becoming increasingly popular, particularly among home gardeners and organic producers. Heirloom plants tend to produce more interesting and flavorful crops at the cost of disease resistance and productivity. Though the definition of an heirloom tomato is vague, they typically refer to tomatoes that have been bred true for 40 years or more.

Photo: A selection of heirloom tomatoes, courtesy of Stu Spivack.

If you've never tasted an heirloom tomato before, to put it simply, you've never tasted a tomato!

The Work to Restore Bobwhite Quail in Appalachia

CHARLESTON, WV – The bobwhite quail, also known as Virginia quail (Colinus virginianus) is a ground-dwelling bird whose territory stretches from Canada, through the United States and into Mexico and the Caribbean.

The bird's name is derived from its characteristic whistling call which sounds like it is screaming, "bob-WHITE" or "bob-bob-WHITE". The syllables are slow and widely spaced, rising in pitch a full octave from beginning to end. Other calls include lisps, peeps, and more rapidly whistled warning calls.

At the turn of the previous century, bobwhite quail were a staple of life in America's eastern mountain range – the birds' elusive nature made it a popular favorite for recreational hunting.

A 1916 issue of *Outing Magazine* described a typical bobwhite hunt:

"Now, my good friend, after you have had what we call a day's hunt, do you not agree with me when I say that the man who essays to bag Bob White must search for him diligently and hunt him intelligently, unless he is willing to go home empty handed?

"Bob White is a gentleman of caprices and an excellent weather prophet… there are times when we hunt the likely places in vain. He may be in the woods after some particular kind of mast which he thinks his constitution requires or it may be ants or eggs. Sometimes we find him in the most unlikely places where so far as we can see there is nothing which he can eat or drink. It may happen to you, to hunt all day until your dogs are discouraged and you yourself are inclined to be ill tempered toward them when about two hours before sundown you fall into a brier grown ditch and flush a covey and then have some shooting which you shall remember all the days of your life…

"These things and many more will happen to you and you will have bad days and good days and you will get heavy in the barrel and sprung in the knees,

but whenever you feel the fall tang in the air and the ragweed begins to wilt, when the cry of the wild geese overhead rings in your ears and the red leaves come showering down, you will feel the call that draws you to the pleasant upland fields where Bob White is king."

Hunting for bobwhite is now a thing of the past in Appalachia, however, a perfect storm of habitat degradation, severe weather and additional factors have contributed to the northern bobwhite population in eastern North America declining by roughly 85% from 1966–2014. This population decline is apparently range-wide and continuing.

In an effort to restore the population, West Virginia Governor Jim Justice announced in early March that the West Virginia Division of Natural Resources is beginning a five-year project to restore northern bobwhite quail to the state.

The bird is a native species and once was found across West Virginia, but the winters of 1977, 1978, and 1979 devastated the bobwhite quail in West Virginia and the numbers simply have not come back.

"There's no question we've lost favorable habitat to quail over the last several decades, however, there is still a significant amount of habitat for quail to flourish by starting this reintroduction program," Gov. Justice said. "Over the next few years, we're going to work so that our folks can once again hear that familiar bobwhite whistle."

West Virginia's Division of Natural Resources (DNR) is working on a restoration project at the Tomblin Wildlife Management Area in Logan County, enhancing habitat that will sustain bobwhite quail. Much of that work has been completed, and the DNR is working closely with the Texas Parks and Wildlife agency on this project.

In February of this year, 48 birds were captured in Texas and released at the Tomblin WMA. Transmitters have been placed on some of the quail to monitor survival and habitat use.

"The DNR is charged with maintaining and protecting West Virginia's Wildlife, committing staff and resources to help restore a species that has been in dramatic decline for over forty years fits right into our mission," said West Virginia DNR Director Stephen McDaniel.

"[Gov. Justice] asked me to look into the possibility of restoring bobwhite quail in West Virginia a couple of years ago so we started working with our friends in Texas to put something together, but the weather never seemed to cooperate until now. We are really excited to get this project underway and the Tomblin WMA is a great place to start," Director McDaniel added.

"We are already providing habitat management resources in the area for our Elk restoration efforts that will benefit these birds as well," he said. "In the future wouldn't it be great if you were able to see both Elk and

Quail on a visit to southern West Virginia?"

"Most game biologists know that the wild populations of quail have been greatly diminished in West Virginia," said Michael Peters, DNR Game Bird and Small Game Project Leader. "With the support of Gov. Justice, we have the interest, financial backing, and support that will allow this long-term, management-intensive project to succeed."

Peters estimates it will take several years to see if this project is successful, although the goal is a self-sustaining population. In the meantime, the information the DNR gathers from this project may allow staff to help private landowners and small farmers to manage bobwhite on their own properties.

"It's kind of neat when you start talking to the older generation. The bobwhite whistle is one of the most common calls they remember," Peters said. "When we get into this project, it would be nice in the years to come if folks all across West Virginia can hear the pleasant bobwhite whistle again in the Mountain State."

Do It Yourself: Expert Help for Improving Bobwhite Habitat on Your Land
Justin Folks, United States Department of Agriculture

The northern bobwhite is often referred to as an "edge" species, seeking habitat where crop fields intersect with woodlands, pastures and abandoned lands. NRCS photo by Stephen Kirkpatrick.

If you're looking to save money around the house, you can find hundreds of helpful videos on a wide variety of "do it yourself" repair and remodeling projects. Social media and other online networking tools can put you in touch with experts to answer your questions along the way.

Well, wildlife habitat can be DIY, too. As a partner biologist with USDA's Natural Resources Conservation Service (NRCS), I work one-on-one with landowners in Virginia to help them make wildlife-friendly improvements to their property, specifically improvements that benefit the northern bobwhite and associated species.

The northern bobwhite, known as the "Prince of Game Birds," was once a familiar face in rural landscapes through much of North America. Habitat loss and fragmentation have caused the bird's numbers to dip by about 80 percent over the last 60 years. Bobwhites depend on early successional habitat, such as (old fields and young, shrubby forests).

Landowners have a great opportunity to help this species as much of bird's potential habitat falls on private lands. The first thing that I tell landowners is creating top-notch habitat for bobwhite isn't costly or complex.

Before you hop on the tractor, fire up a chainsaw or fill up a backpack sprayer, you need to have a good understanding of the species' biology and habitat requirements. Bobwhite quail are a boom-and-bust species. They pair up in spring and summer but live in groups the rest of the year. They roost in rings on the ground and have an average life expectancy of only six to eight months.

More often than not, landowners have a great native seedbank and just need to add a couple of habitat management practices to get things moving in the right direction. In other cases, they may be actively trying to manage for quail but need to tweak their approach.

This field full of wildflowers not only provides great habitat for bobwhite but for pollinators, too! Photo by Justin Folks.

"Bobs" need three types of interconnected cover: nesting, brooding and escape, and the primary reason for their decline is habitat loss and fragmentation. While the critters might be complex, managing their habitat doesn't have to be — simple steps like mowing in March instead of October or leaving the edges of a crop field fallow can make your land useable for quail.

I have been on many site visits where I know the landowner has a pretty good idea of what quail need, but he or she may not be the best at reading the land and seeing the opportunities. NRCS and other conservation partners, such as the Virginia Department of Game and Inland Fisheries and Virginia Tech's Conservation Management Institute, provide technical and financial assistance to landowners to help them recognize these opportunities.

Some of the practices that NRCS and partners are helping landowners implement include field borders, hedgerows, conservation cover, filter strips, prescribed burning, and establishing diminished pine species such as shortleaf and longleaf pine.

Managing for bobwhite benefits many other wildlife species, including songbirds, pollinators, rabbits, wild turkey and deer. It may take a while for quail to respond to your efforts, but the impacts are immediate for these other species. Enjoy the "fringe benefits" of conservation work!

Remember if we each do a little, it adds up.

If you're interested in learning more, I encourage you to contact your local USDA service center to learn about assistance available through Farm Bill conservation programs.

Another resource for you to check out is Bargain Basement Bobwhites: An Affordable DIY Approach to Managing Land for Wild Bobwhite Quail that I worked on with the Virginia Quail and Early Succession Species Recovery Initiative.

Coming 2024: Total Solar Eclipse

On August 21, 2017, our family traveled to Sweetwater, Tennessee, a small community of 5,700+ residents nestled at the foothills of the Smoky Mountains. Prior to 2017, our family had never even heard of this quiet East Tennessee community located along US Route 11, however, in the third week of August, we found ourselves racing thousands of other motorists who – like us – were descending upon the community.

Our "Sweetwater or Bust" mentality had absolutely nothing to do with anything located within the jurisdictional boundaries of the community, but instead, our attention was focused toward the heavens.

Thanks to astrological luck eons in the making, Sweetwater, Tennessee, was positioned directly in the path of what the media had dubbed the Great American Eclipse, a total solar eclipse which stretched from the Pacific Ocean to the Atlantic.

Prior to the 2017 eclipse, no solar eclipse had been visible across the entire United States since June 8, 1918, and not since the February 1979 eclipse had a total eclipse been visible from anywhere in the mainland United States.

The event was spectacular and one that I think of often.

As amazing as it was for our family to see such an event, the moon's shadow casting was so much the more wonderful for the community of Sweetwater – a year after the eclipse the townspeople again assembled in the community square to unveil a new town clock that had been purchased with profits garnered from the eclipse.

Local leaders say the event put Sweetwater on the map and provided an opportunity for them to punch outside of their weight class – and they did not squander such an opportunity.

Fast-forward to 2020, nearly three years later, and a countless number of similar communities across the nation are on the doorstep of a very similar opportunity.

On Monday, April 8, 2024, the final total solar eclipse will pass through the continental United States until August 2045.

The 2024 total solar eclipse will be visible in Mexico, United States, and Canada and is being called, "The Great North American Eclipse".

In the United States, totality will be visible through the states of Texas (including parts of San Antonio, Austin, and Fort Worth and all of Arlington, Dallas, Killeen, Temple, Texarkana, Tyler and Waco), Oklahoma, Arkansas (including Hot Springs, Jonesboro, and Little Rock), Missouri, Illinois, Kentucky, Indiana (including Bloomington, Evansville, Indianapolis, Muncie, Terre Haute, and Vincennes), a very small area of Michigan, Ohio (including Akron, Dayton, Lima, Roundhead, Toledo, Cleveland, Warren, Newton Falls and Austintown), Pennsylvania (including

Erie), Upstate New York (including Buffalo, Rochester, Syracuse, the Adirondacks, Potsdam, and Plattsburgh), and northern Vermont (including Burlington), New Hampshire, and Maine, with the line of totality going almost directly over the state's highest point Mount Katahdin, the final step of the Appalachian Trail.

The largest city entirely in the path will be Dallas, Texas.

Totality will, coincidentally, pass through the town of Wapakoneta, Ohio, home of Neil Armstrong, the first person to set foot upon the Moon.

This eclipse will be the first total solar eclipse to be visible from Canada since February 26, 1979, the first in Mexico since July 11, 1991.

It will be the only total solar eclipse in the 21st century where totality is visible in all three of the countries.

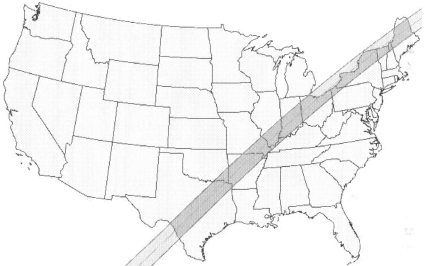

Photo: Pathway of the April 2024, "Great North American Solar Eclipse" in the United States of America.

Managing Snakes in a Residence, Business or Other Occupied Space
Produced by Virginia Cooperative Extension, Virginia Tech

There may be nothing more startling or unsettling to some folks than finding a snake crawling along the baseboard of a room in one's home or finding a shed snake skin in the cellar, bedroom closet, or attic — a clear indicator that a snake has been in the building. Not knowing where the snake is currently or whether it has left the site is enough to drive some people out of the building until they can be assured it is "all clear." To many folks, this is a violation of their personal living or working space.

Snakes enter a building for several primary reasons. In many cases, they simply were following and hunting their preferred food item (mice), which also

Photo: Black Rat Snake, courtesy of Virginia's Shenandoah National Park.

happened to be sharing our living space. In other cases, snakes may be seeking a secure location to lay eggs. Snakes sometimes enter a building seeking conditions that will help them shed their old skin (small openings or sharp angles provide useful wedges to help peel off the old skin). Finally, a snake may seek temporary shelter from a predator or to help regulate body temperature.

Regardless of why a snake may have entered a residence or work area, most people just want to know how to remove it. However, people confronted with a snake must understand that under existing wildlife regulations, it is illegal to kill any species of snake in Virginia unless it presents an imminent threat to one's personal health and safety.

Snakes are classified as nongame species and therefore are afforded full protection under existing nongame regulations, similar to all other species in this category. In the case of the canebrake rattlesnake, which is one of Virginia's state-listed endangered species, neither the animal nor its habitat can be destroyed.

Thus, trying to kill any snake found in the home is not an appropriate solution. Instead, homeowners should concentrate on eliminating the attraction that brought the snake to the home in the first place and closing all points of access that allowed the animal to enter. The following serve as useful steps for homeowners to consider:

1. Eliminate the prey population that snakes are looking for by removing or cleaning up food resources in the home that attract and support rodents. This would include things like spilled bird seed, accessible pet food stores, open containers of dry goods, and similar potential food items. Transfer all stored dry goods to metal or glass containers that can be tightly sealed and cannot be chewed by rodents.

2. Repair, seal, or close off any openings 1/4 inch or larger that provide animals with access to the interior of the building. Most rodents need an opening of only 1/2 inch in size, or access to an opening that they can enlarge by gnawing, to get into buildings. Places to concentrate your initial search efforts would be where utility services (e.g., water, sewer, electric, telephone, cable) enters the home; where the clothes dryer vent exits the building; around doors, windows, and bulkheads to the basement or garage (including the gap under a large garage door); and where the house sits on its foundation (the sill area). Remember, if a rodent can get in, so can a snake —often by using the very same openings.

3. Thin or reduce the amount of landscape plantings that exist immediately against the foundation of the home. Thick, lush gardens and layers of growth located against the home provide perfect cover and protection to both snakes and their prey. Further, thick plantings provide these animals with time under protective cover to look for new ways to get in without having to worry about being exposed or vulnerable.

If you should find a snake in the home, removal can be accomplished most easily by using long-handled implements, such as a flat-bladed shovel, scoop, or broom, to pick up the animal or sweep it into a deep container that has been laid on its side. It is possible to scoop up some snakes with a large-bladed shovel and physically carry them outdoors.

Individuals who have experience in handling snakes may be able to catch a nonvenomous snake by grabbing it immediately behind the head and carrying it outside. Wear gloves and a long-sleeved garment to reduce the likelihood of sustaining a bite. If there is any uncertainty about the identity of the snake, do not attempt to catch or handle the snake.

If a snake is suspected to be present, but is not immediately evident — or has gone into hiding before capture was possible — several options exist for homeowners. Snakes often will seek cover where warmth and humidity exist, such as around large appliances (e.g., washers, dryers, freezers, hot water heaters, or furnaces) and computers and display monitors. A loosely clumped bath towel that has been lightly dampened and placed near an appliance where a snake is suspected of hiding sometimes will entice the snake to crawl out and move under the towel. If you are ready with capture tools, you often can sweep up the unsuspecting animal as you quickly lift the towel.

A capture device known as a glue board or glue box is available commercially and sometimes can be used to lure a difficult-to-catch snake from the hiding spot. A glue box for snakes is a long, rectangular, cardboard box with an opening at each end and an interior floor that has been coated with a strong adhesive. A snake that enters the box looking for cover becomes entangled in the glue and usually cannot remove itself. For especially large snakes, several rodent glue boards attached securely to a wooden plank and placed against an inner wall may be effective. Glue devices may provide an opportunity to capture and remove a difficult-to-catch animal using other means.

However, never throw a box or a modified glue board that contains a snake directly into the trash. This is a tremendously inhumane act that will result in a very slow death for the animal, and it is illegal.

Further, the people who process your trash might be exposed to potential danger should the animal's head remain free or it manages to free itself from the device while in the trash receptacle.

Once you have moved the container outside and away from the home, you can easily free the animal by pouring a very small amount of vegetable oil over the surface of the glue to neutralize its stickiness. The snake will be able to wriggle itself free.

Snakes in a Yard, Activity Area, or Public Space

The most effective way to minimize or prevent a chance encounter with a snake outdoors is to modify the habitat such that the snake no longer can fulfill its basic life needs easily. Basic life needs, in this case, refer to food, water, cover, and space. By manipulating the habitat around your home, you can make it difficult fora snake to survive there. Examples of actions that might be taken include:

1. Eliminate, remove, or relocate brush piles, refuse, stored building products, stacked firewood, or other materials that may provide useful cover and hiding spots for both snakes and the prey species they hunt.

2. Thin out or selectively remove weedy or overgrown patches of vegetation that may harbor small prey animals such as rodents and provide cover for hiding snakes.

3. In areas where small children or pets play, keep the grass well-mowed and maintain an expanse of well-cropped vegetation between the play area and the surrounding woods. Snakes usually do not like to be exposed in the open and away from cover.

4. To create a snake-free play area, encircle the area to be protected with a fine-meshed (1/8- to 1/4-inch)fence, about 36 inches in height, that has been dug into the ground so that no gaps exist (figure 5). The fence should be supported by stout posts driven into the ground on the inside of the protected area, but angled outward at about 30 degrees. Because of the outward slant of this design, any access gates incorporated in the fence must open inward. Some fencing experts recommend leaving extra fence material at the top of the device such that it can fold over to the outside of the fence and hang loosely at the top as an additional means of preventing the snake from getting over the top. Be sure that no vegetation comes in contact with or close to the fence as it may provide a means for access over the fence. Remember: snakes generally are skilled climbers.

Repellents

A number of commercially available products have been registered by the U.S. Environmental Protection Agency (EPA) for use as snake repellents. All of the currently registered products contain some combination of pulverized sulfur and naphthalene as active ingredients, and most are offered in a shakable powder or granular formulation. However, research conducted to investigate the effectiveness of these active ingredients has not demonstrated success in repelling snakes.

In its effort to eradicate the brown tree snake (Boigairregularis), an especially troublesome exotic snake introduced into a number of Pacific Island ecosystems, the U.S. Department of Agriculture, Animal Plant and Health Inspection Service, Wildlife Services (USDA-APHIS-WS), investigated use of new snake repellents based on formulations containing mixtures of essential oils, including cinnamon, clove, and/or eugenol. Although hopes were high of discovering an effective repellent using these oils, field research proved otherwise (Kraus et al. 2015).

Recent research (Gallagher et al. 2017) examined the effectiveness of Milorganite, a reprocessed biosolid produced from municipal sewer sludge, as a snake repellent. Preliminary results from controlled field testing suggest that a repellent effect was detected on the species of snake used in testing (Eastern rat snake), but further research was needed before this approach could be recommended.

Readers are reminded that use of any other ingredients or "home-brewed" snake repellents made from material for which an EPA product registration does not exist is a violation of federal law.

Granny Myers' Curse

Written by Henry W. Shoemaker
First appeared in Pennsylvania Mountain Stories in 1907

That belief in witchcraft still exists in the United States cannot be denied as the newspapers every now and then print accounts of doings of alleged witches in remote parts of the country. But nowhere does it flourish and its teachings defy the advance of modern enlightenment to such an extent as in the mountains of central Pennsylvania.

A typical case of Pennsylvania witchcraft is that of an old Swiss, Christ, by name, who tills a sixty-acre farm on a bleak mountain top along what is known as the Pine Road that runs from Jersey Shore to Loganton. His house stands back a hundred yards from the road.

The original structure was built of logs but as more prosperous days ensued, a frame mansion was tacked on the less imposing log cabin. Not another house can be seen from the windows which look over a dreary expanse of fire swept summits, slashings, and abandoned clearings. The gable of the large barn standing between the road and the house is covered with bear paws nailed in disorderly profusion. Several sets of buskhorns adorn the slanting roof of the nearby corncrib.

With such surrounding it is not surprising that people became easy prey to mental vagaries and live in terror of persons possessing supposed supernatural powers.

Formerly, Christ had his brother Michael, whose house was two miles up a secluded hemlock hollow for next door neighbor, but alleged spirit rapping and apparitions, culminating in the suicide of an old man named Righter, who made his home with the family, caused Mike to move to a farm nearer town and neighbors.

At present, Christ's nearest neighbors are the family of an old woman whom we shall call Granny Myers reputed among the mountaineers as a witch and famed for the potency of her spells who lived in windowless shanty three miles away.

One Fall, about ten years ago, some of Christ's cattle broke into the Myers buckwheat field and one was mysteriously shot. Threats of criminal prosecution were made until one night Granny Myers strode into Christ's kitchen and in the presence of several witnesses cursed the farmer, his wife, and daughter in these words, "Christ, you shall shrivel to death with rheumatics, your woman shall develop a cancer, and your daughter shall cough up blood until she fades away."

Then she went out, slamming the door after her, leaving the Christs in a state of nervous collapse. Several months passed by, it was the month of February, the Pine Road was deep in snow and not even a shingle sled could navigate, but a little thing like this could not daunt old John Dice, the witch doctor from the river bottom, who, clad in his familiar coat of Confederate gray, knee deep in slush was bound for a vendue in the east end of Sugar Valley.

As he passed the Christ farm, a withered figure hobbled to the fence and waved his hand at him. "Shon, come here," he called.

"My woman is dying mit der cancer, my girl is coughing up blood and I'm dying mit der rheumatics."

The witch doctor climbed the gate and followed the farmer to his house. Mrs. Christ, complaining of terrible pains in her side, lay moaning on a sofa and the nineteen year old daughter worn almost to a skeleton, dragged herself about the house coughing every few minutes.

"Granny Myers done it," was all they would say. The witch doctor, who understood the trouble at a glance, promised to have the spell removed within the week, and before an hour was at the hut of the alleged witch.

On his way, in a snow covered lot, he noticed four miserable horses huddled together, protecting themselves as best they could from the cruel winter wind. All told they had but two eyes and one good tail among them, these cast offs from the dispersal sale of the Williamport Traction Company—now operated by trolley.

Granny Myers, a tall rawboned woman with a long nose and enormous hands, was smoking her clay pipe by the stove, when her old enemy, who never knocked, came in, shaking the snow from his boots.

"Go over to Christ's and tell them you have taken that spell off, or mark my word, it's now Friday, by next Monday your four horses will be dead, and you will follow them."

That was all John Dice said before he resumed his tramp to the vendue. The next Monday, true to his promise, he appeared at Granny Myers's door a scythe and a poleaxe, purchased at the vendue, slung over his massive shoulders. Granny heard his footsteps and was on hand to meet him.

"You old deil," said she, "meh crowbates are all four dead, and I wus to Christ's a yesterday."

When the witch doctor revisited the Christ kitchen a vastly different scene met his eyes. Christ, humming to himself, was mending a rocking-chair; his smiling wife lifting a heavy kettle from the stove, while his buxom daughter was setting the tea table.

"Vont you stay to supper, Shon?" said Christ, "the old hex's taken off the spell, an we're ahl well again."

Witchcraft vs. Mother in Law

Ranny Myers had a daughter who was "mahried" to Jakey Welshans, a small storekeeper in the German Settlement. The old woman would tie up her bundle and wend her way over the hills and make protracted visits to her daughter, often lasting a year at a time, much to the disgust of Jakey.

On one of these visits, when she had created turmoil among the Welshans for eleven months and showed no signs of going home, Jakey hit upon the scheme of enlisting the aid of John Dice in ridding his household of the disturbing mother-in-law.

So one day he met John who was electioneering for a Republican candidate. Jakey is a Democrat and told him of his unhappy predicament.

"Der old voman is awful scaret of you, Shon," ever since you kilt them horses on her and if you tell her somethin bad may come to her she'll light out preddy quick."

"All right," said John, "lets tend to her case now."

"Der old voman is a great lisdener, Shon," continued Jakey, "and if you talks kinder loud on der porch she'll be peekin through der keyhole."

Arriving at the Welshans store, they walked around to the side porch ostensibly to give John a drink from the well. A hasty glance through the kitchen window showed Granny Myers standing inside the closed kitchen door.

"I'm down on that infernal mother-in-law of yours," said John, in his loudest tones and she'd better be going home soon or—"

"Oh, don't speak like dot, Shon, she's a loafly voman," interposed son-in-law Jakey.

"I mean what I say," said John, "I have no use for that old hex, and she'd better clear out, for if she doesn't, her blood will dry in her veins and she'll die standing up."

Then John got his drink of well water and resumed his electioneering for the Republican candidate. But his words had their effect.

At the dinner table that day, Granny said she "thought it was time to go home." All prevailed upon her to stay, even the children, but with no avail.

At half past four the next morning she came downstairs with her bundles and started on her ten mile walk across the mountains.

And to this day, Granny Myers has never revisited the German Settlement.

The Crucifixion Legend of the Dogwood Tree
Appalachian Magazine

Photo: Dogwood flower, courtesy of Steve Karg

Billions of people around the globe will pause this spring to remember the Cross of Calvary, as well the miracle of resurrection. Celebrations will begin early in the week leading up to the Holy Day and continue until the last observations of Easter are concluded in the westernmost islands of the South Pacific late-Sunday evening.

For many, this particular Sunday will mark the most sacred date on the Christian calendar as it serves as a reminder of the tortuous death Christ endured in an effort to purchase lost souls in need of salvation, as well as death's unconditional surrender to Christ, the Savior who arose three days later as a victor o'er the dark domain of hell.

Central to all observations this week, whether Protestant or Catholic, is the simple yet extraordinarily recognizable symbol of Christianity: The Roman Cross of Calvary.

Whether printed, trimmed in gold and worn as jewelry or affixed to a steeple, the cross is one of the most recognizable symbols on the planet and serves as a timeless reminder of Christianity.

Speaking of the cross long before his crucifixion, Jesus proclaimed to his followers, "he that taketh not his cross, and followeth after me, is not worthy of me," in Mark 10.38.

After Christ's death and resurrection, the Apostle Paul mentioned the cross, stating, "For the preaching of the cross is to them that perish foolishness; but unto us which are saved it is the power of God."

There is no question that the cross is important to Christianity, but there is great debate as to what the cross was actually made from.

Today, many Biblical scholars believe there is evidence that it was constructed of a combination of cedar, pine and cypress, a nod to the prophecy of Isaiah which stated, "The glory of Lebanon shall come unto thee, the fir tree [cedar], the pine tree, and the box [cypress] together, to beautify the place of my sanctuary; and I will make the place of my feet glorious."

Despite these thoughts, there is an old tale not based in Biblical texts but instead in oral tradition that found its way to me when I was just a young child in the mountains of Appalachia.

One afternoon while walking through the woods alongside my father, we came upon an out of place dogwood tree, Virginia's official State Tree.

Grabbing its limbs, my dad gave it a good tug and proclaimed to me, "This is the type of tree Jesus was hung on."

"How do you know?" I asked inquisitively.

"That's what all the old people have told me my entire life," he answered, as we continued on our march through the woods.

A few days later, he brought me branch of the tree and recounted a legend I found strangely fascinating.

"Dogwoods used to be far bigger and stronger than they are today, but after one was cut down and made into the cross that Jesus died on, they became cursed to forever be small and weak."

Handing me one of the blooms from the tree, he continued, "Take a look at the white flower — anytime you see this, you are to remember the cross. Do you see the nail marks in the flower? Look at the red crown of thorns. Break that red berry and see the blood…"

My father was not a particularly religious man while I was growing up, but holding that dogwood limb knee to knee with him revealed something I never before realized — despite his use of words my mother would wash my mouth out with soap for using, my father held a great respect for the Jesus my mother made sure my sister and me worshipped each Sunday at our local church.

As I've grown older and a bit more cynical in my adult life regarding the authenticity of legends and folklore, I can't say that I still truly believe the story of the Dogwood as my father presented it to me — the Bible is mute when it comes to the type of tree Jesus was crucified upon so I guess I will be too — but I can say that I will forever cherish this precious memory of hearing my father talk about the Cross of Jesus.

Whether it was made from a Dogwood, Cedar, Pine or some other tree, the contents of the cross are not nearly as important as its message:

"And, having made peace through the blood of his cross, by him to reconcile all things unto himself; by him, I say, whether they be things in earth, or things in heaven." — Colossians 1.20

—Part Four—
Random Musings & My Two Cents

"Spring Has Sprung"

—Part Four—
Random Musings & My Two Cents

My Two Cents: Reader & Writer Notes
Losing Our Appalachian Mountain– Pg. 111
Trappers– Pg. 116
Submission from 94-Year-Old Writer – Pg. 125
If this Old House Could Talk:
The Henry Jackson Homestead in Upshur County, W.Va.– Pg. 131
Poetry from the Carolina Mountains – Pg. 128

—*Featured*—
Does Appalachia Need a Flag?– Pg. 120

Are you a writer? Do you have a story to tell?

We would love to take a look at your work and consider publishing you in the "Random Musings & My Two Cents" section of Appalachian Magazine!

Here's what you need to do:

Send a copy of your article (in pdf or Word format) to the following email address: **themountainwriter@gmail.com**

If we're able to publish your work, you will receive a complimentary copy of that quarter's edition of the print publication!

"Spring Has Sprung"

Losing Our Appalachian Mountain
Written by Mary Whalen

Mary Whalen is a retired nurse and teacher who lives with her husband on a chicken farm in Northern Kentucky. Her article, "Predator-Proof Chicken Coop", has appeared in Backwoods Home Magazine, May/June 2016

In 2017 Mary Whalen submitted an article to Appalachian Magazine for publishing. Unfortunately, we made a mistake and attributed the article. Since the article was so wonderful, we thought we'd include it again — this time with the correct attribution.

In the fall of '96, when the crisp leaves of the oak and ash and walnut and hickory trees were turning red, orange, and brown, and the smell of bonfires spoke of the end of hot summer nights, my husband lost his job and we lost our church, in the same month.

Don't ask me to explain the church incident. It turned into a blessing and a healing though, because with our foundations cracked, we found ourselves suddenly able to gratify a long abandoned wanderlust. We left our home in Cincinnati, to explore the mountains of southeastern Kentucky.

We needed solace.

We enjoyed lunch at a small town, and on a local realtor's tip, we bounced along a one-lane overgrown trail forgotten by time and happened upon—a mountain.

We did a little research. It was a peak in the Appalachian basin, sometimes called the hill country, but anything I have to crane my head back and not see the top of, is a mountain to me. It rose above a stream with a pasture of gently rolling spurs drawn up to coniferous peaks. An old decrepit barn stood sentry near the stream.

We'd heard from the realtor that bear, red fox, deer and rattlesnake were the only inhabitants of this property. We found out differently.

After giving us uncertain directions, the realtor explained that it would be best if we were friendly to everyone we met as "you don't want to cross anyone, you know what I mean?" We weren't really sure what he'd meant.

The mountain was covered with logged over rutted roads that seemed too narrow for our Tracker to navigate. We also discovered from the deeps of the forested trails, that at three o'clock in the afternoon, it looked like the sun was about to set. At three o'clock in the afternoon!

My husband, John, is of Scots-Irish descent whose relatives originally came from Scotland to County Waterford, Ireland in the 17th century and thence by way of New York, to Kentucky He has inherited this spirit of adventure. He's a hardworking man who doesn't know when to quit. I could see the wheels turning in his mind, thinking of all the things he would do with this property. Maybe start marking trees so we could widen one of the many roads on the mountain, or build a small cabin.

We headed back to town and bought the place.

This is where we got stuck!

The next day, we came back and headed up the widest road on the mountain, noting bear tracks in the dirt, when suddenly our little green Tracker sank into a ditch the size of Manhattan. Upon walking down to the flat area by the stream, we heard a car coming down another road on the other side of the mountain.

It was a small car driven by a very young couple. The young lady in the front passenger seat was holding an infant in her arms.

"What's the problem?" the fella asked. We explained our dilemma and directly, the girl handed me the infant and said they would be back with help. Here I was in the growing dusk, in a place I didn't know, holding a baby I didn't know. Maybe it wasn't true that mountain people were not friendly.

Not ten minutes later, we heard sound of machinery coming from other side of the creek. Sure enough, the couple brought help in the form of a tractor and a strong looking red headed driver.

Our car was freed from the ruts in minutes. My husband offered some of the fallen trees left over from logging, as a gesture of appreciation. Our young savior offered his hand and smiled. "Name's Smith," he said before roaring away in a blue cloud of tractor smoke.

The young girl matter-of-factly took the baby back from my arms, and away they went too.

Even as dusk was upon us, we figured that we still had time to travel past our mountain in an opposite direction from the road we came in on, when we noticed a older fellow heading our way through the tall grass by the barn. He was a wiry, spare man, wearing a slouched, tan hat.

We hollered "Hello!" No answer.

As he got nearer, John extended his hand, said hello again, and introduced himself, explaining why we were there. When John mentioned our realtor's name, the man, who acknowledged his name as Will, gave us a half smile, and shook John's hand.

"I'm the only neighbor you'd have around here", he explained, eyeing us up and down. "I keep a lookout on all this property." I put on my friendliest smile.

We talked for awhile and he suggested that we drive on past his house down the road "a piece". "You'll see where I live. You'll also find a mighty old post office but it ain't used anymore", he said.

Our interest piqued, we crossed the creek again and turned left and there was his cabin. It had a large front porch, and a scattering of chickens clucking their way around the front yard, and there on the porch were

several rockers. On one sat a woman that must have been his wife, and on another sat an even older lady, a wizened matriarch it seemed, with iron gray hair in a bun.

There were several children of various sizes hanging around the porch, all grinning and waving to beat the band. If we'd been mountain folks already, we'd have gotten out and said hello. I reflected that city people need to be initiated in the art of neighborliness.

We waved back, while driving slowly down the graveled road.

The road became narrower as we went along. A mile or two later, the gravel became a desolate creek bed. There was nowhere else to turn, and no other road, so we continued on. The creek bed became a dead end. No post office in sight, in fact, no road left at all. If we hadn't had this small car that took us twenty minutes to turn around in, we would still be there. I wondered if even God knew where we were.

With the approach of deep evening shadows, we once again passed Will's house on the right, and we could see that they were on the porch, still rocking, still grinning, the kids still laughing, and the chickens still clucking. Well we laughed right back. We'd been had. I loved that our neighbors had a sense of humor. Being able to share a laugh over something with someone makes me feel welcome.

On subsequent visits, before actually investing in materials to build a small cabin, we explored and tramped around the mountain and also explored our growing friendship with our neighbors. We planted turnips in the field by the creek, at our new neighbor's suggestion, to attract the deer, both for our neighbors and ourselves' sustenance.

Over the next few weeks, we found our new adventures in the hills positively rapturous, —we also found we had an unexpected, exorbitant tax bill from the city we left behind that we had no money for. It seems that when you sell a house in a populated area in the big city, and plunk down a much smaller amount in a rural, mountainous area, the Federal government steps rights up to claim their due.

We had to sell the mountain property. It hurt.

We and our neighbor and his kindly wife, whom we officially met on our second foray into this wilderness, exchanged letters and greeting cards over the next few years.

After a while, we lost touch. We never went back.

We thought of it.

We had learned first-hand something of Appalachian culture, and people. We loved the warm embrace of mountain ridges that spoke of history and strife and of a type of strength and resiliency not known to city folks. I felt safe there. We had fallen in love with the people. Their pioneering spirit resonated with ours.

It's been twenty years, and it still stings when it comes to mind what we lost.

Eventually we found a farm in a spot nearer to northern Kentucky and raised a bunch of cattle, goats, sheep, and most numerous of all, chickens. We learned to live off the land, but never forgot our first dream of living in the mountains, and understanding a people that settled our country. It was the adventure we almost had.

Would it look the same to me if we went back someday? Maybe, but I think my heart would ache.

Since then, I have studied more about the Appalachian people; their unique struggles and heartwarming graciousness. I wish I was one of them.

Share this article with your friends on Facebook:

Trappers

Written by Gary Fadley

From Cresaptown, Maryland, near Cumberland, the author is a father, grandfather, firefighter, life-members of Vietnam Veterans of America, and the proud husband of retired Master Sergeant Cynthia Bray, USMC.

Growing up in the 1960's in a large, poor family in Mountain Maryland, on the Potomac River, which separates the state from West Virginia, my older brother and I were obliged to help our father feed the family by fishing, trapping, frog gigging, and turtle bobbing. We delivered death to a lot of God's creatures. But it was always more out of necessity than sport.

We ate the meat, and we sold the furs.

We did not eat the fish from the very polluted Potomac River, however. We had known the river's reputation and foul odor even before the U.S. EPA recognized the paper mill upstream at Luke, Maryland as one of the state's largest polluters. Additionally, the acid draining from abandoned coal mines, and even waste water from homes, was continuously pouring into the river.

However, my father and others reasoned that, even though we could not eat the fish from the river, we could still eat its frogs and turtles because they didn't have gills, meaning they were not "breathing" the water. I didn't understand the science behind the logic, but I trusted my father's wisdom in such matters. And I remember looking forward to a dinner of delicious fried turtle taken from the river, or fish or frogs from one of the many ponds in Western Maryland and West Virginia.

My first memory of trapping was created when I was five or six years old, on a snowy morning that Dad decided to take his youngest son along to check the box traps, which capture the rabbits alive. Dad was soon trudging through a foot of snow. And I tried to step in the giant tracks he made.

We discovered an unfortunate, big-eared victim in the first trap we checked that morning.

The creature might well have been a plump, full-grown rabbit intended for the dinner table, but to me he was a fluffy little bunny, and I wanted to hold him and take him home. But, before I could even touch him, Dad gave him a karate chop on the back of his neck, and he went to sleep. And I didn't like that, but I got over it soon enough, and I understood very early that some animals would have to die in order for us to eat.

My favorite thing to catch was the turtles, which we caught in the sport we called "turtle bobbing," in which we'd put walnut-size chunks of beef on large hooks that we tied to lengths of chalk-line. We'd place the beef-baited hooks in the water at the edge of the Potomac River or around a pond, and we'd tie the other ends of the lines to trees, stumps, or rocks.

We'd put these lines out just as the sun was going down, and we'd return right at sunrise to check them, at which time we'd typically have two, three, or four large turtles to angrily greet us.

A large turtle wants to fight about being captured, and they have the snapping power to relieve you of your fingers, so the process of getting them out of the water and into burlap sacks is dangerously exciting and absolutely fun. Not only was the turtle the most exciting creature to catch; he was also the one that tasted best after Mom fried his powerful and delicious legs and neck muscles.

So, among other things, we were trappers, but we were not really trappers when compared with Harry Bammers, a guy who always comes to mind when I think of trapping.

Harry Bammers was an old friend of Dad's from Virginia, a rugged mountain of a mountain man.

I remember only three or four times in my life that Harry Bammers came to our house, a five-room bungalow on Haystack Mountain, and I had the impression that he had probably been in any house only three or four times. This guy was a real-life mountain man—a trapper. And I think the only times he ever stopped at our house was when he had been passing by while on his way to market with a load of pelts. I only saw his panel truck a few times in my life, but, each time, it was loaded with hundreds of furs and skins that unfortunate creatures no longer needed after Harry Bammers wrung their necks or clubbed the life out of them.

Harry Bammers was very large and very loud. He had long, dirty hair and a big, black, bushy beard. He dressed in many layers of raggedy clothes, and he smelled like kerosene, whiskey, and animals. Everything was large about this man—even his whiskey bottle. My dad's bottles were usually smaller, flat-shaped things, but Harry Bammer's bottles were big and round—just like Harry Bammers.

As far as I can reckon, the only reason this boar of a man ever stopped at our house was to drink with Dad, do some loud talking, ogle my mother and sisters, and then go back to his business of mass murder and mutilation, a business at which I knew him to be proficient, for I had peered in through the rear window of his ugly panel-truck, which was heavy-laden with the remains of hapless creatures whose final misfortune was an encounter with Harry Bammers.

Out of the few times that Harry Bammers had disturbed our peace by only his presence, one time in particular stands out in memory. It was an autumn visit in the tenth year of my life, and it was almost certainly before trapping season, but regulated "seasons" are for sportsmen who obey laws, and no one ever accused this boorish blackguard of being a sportsman. Harry Bammers and my father were sitting at the kitchen table drinking from that big bottle, and they were the only ones in that kitchen, because no doubt the rest of us had retreated from the disturbing presence of this bloated guest. I was in the "boys' room," which was adjacent to the kitchen and was the room I shared with my brother, who was asleep on his bed that warm, Indian summer evening. Our room was not blessed with a door, but a curtain hung in the doorway between the kitchen and our bedroom.

I think I went into the kitchen to get a drink of water I didn't really need, but the real reason was that I just had to have another look at this frightening, disturbing visitor. And who can understand a child's sometimes-morbid attraction to all things scary? But soon after I entered the kitchen, Harry Bammers began to comment to Dad about me, saying something about my having been "only a baby" the last time he had seen me. Then, though I've never understood the repulsion that must have been from intuition alone, I was quickly out through the screen door and into the bountiful and refreshing air of Appalachian fall, having virtually fled from the presence Harry Bammers.

Curiosity, however, can be dangerously powerful, so I was very quickly behind the house, peering through a window at a kitchen table where sat my mostly-reasonable father and the unfathomable savage who was bigger even than the bears whose furs he had wrested from lifeless, conquered bodies.

The window through which I peered was actually the window of my own room, the boys' room, but that room was next to the kitchen, and the curtain that hung between the boys' room and the kitchen was partly open, so my view was through the boys' room and into the kitchen, and my brother lay on the bed next to the window, apparently asleep, exhausted from a day of bringing coal and wood into the basement in preparation for the coming winter. I had arrived there at my stealthy position with such haste that Harry Bammers had not quite finished talking about me. With only a window screen and several feet between us, I again heard him say something about how big I was. And a skinny boy with a big brother would normally enjoy a remark about his being "big," unless that remark indicated that he had attracted the attention of a large predator. Still, however, even though I could not accept a compliment from Harry Bammers, I was oddly glad he had said it, and I hoped it made my father proud.

But my hopes were soon dashed when Dad said, "That aint nothing. Look at this other one," as he pulled back the curtain to the boy's room to show off his biggest son, who was lying uncovered in the autumn heat, wearing only briefs. "Look how big this one is," Dad said, "and look at how big his legs are."

That's all I remember of the conversation between these two Virginians, who soon went back to pouring shots from that over-sized bottle. I think my moment of jealousy toward my brother was soon replaced by my readiness to defend him, feeling that his uncovered body should not have been brought to the attention of Harry Bammers. This feeling, however, was no fault of this mountain man. But by then I had already been the victim of men who were predators of boys instead of animals. And I'm afraid I had already begun to generalize, giving way to unfounded suspicions and the beginnings of an unhelpful distrust of others.

The reader, however, should not conclude that my father had been reckless or irresponsible in his having Harry Bammers in the family home, or even in his drinking whiskey there with him. It was not irresponsibility but confidence that allowed Dad to take advantage of the mountain man's whiskey, or perhaps even to bless Harry Bammers with a measure of friendship. He was confident, that is, that he could beat the devil out of Harry Bammers if necessary. Dad wore his sleeves rolled up, displaying his biceps like a gunslinger displays twin six-guns, and his fists had their own share of Appalachian history from the Blue Ridge

Mountains of Virginia to the Eastern Alleghenies of Western Maryland, where sat a little red house on the side of a mountain called Haystack.

—Featured—
Does Appalachia Need a Flag?
Written by Appalachian Magazine

With origins that date back to antiquity and being mentioned in the Bible, the importance of flags dates back thousands of years.

If one thinks that hoisting a piece of fabric up a pole is an outdated tradition from a bygone era, they should think again, as flags – more than ever before – are capable of eliciting extreme emotion, even in the year 2020.

They also work to identify us with various groups, much larger than ourselves. Whether it is for the good or the bad, flags have a way of drawing out reaction in people who otherwise would be void of feeling. *Old Glory*, the *Confederate Flag*, a *Swastika*, the *Rainbow Pride Flag*, the *Christian Flag*, the *Gadsen Flag* ("Don't Tread on Me"), even a *Canadian Flag* are all used by "tribes" to send loud and clear messages as to which group they belong.

In 2006 the North American Vexillological Association published a pamphlet entitled, *Good Flag, Bad Flag: How to Design a Great Flag.*

The short handbook provided five basic principles to create an outstanding flag for organizations, cities, tribes of people and even countries. Their rules are concise and understandable:

I. Keep it Simple
The flag should be so simple that a child can draw it from memory . . .

II. Use Meaningful Symbolism
The flag's images, colors, or patterns should relate to what it symbolizes…

III. Use 2-3 Basic Colors
Limit the number of colors on the flag to three, which contrast well and come from the standard color set…

IV. No Lettering or Seals
Never use writing of any kind or an organization's seal…

V. Be Distinctive or be Relatable
Avoid duplicating other flags, but use similarities to show connections.

Unfortunately, in the United States, the vast majority of us live in states that break nearly all of these rules. Hardly any of the state flags are simple, most have upwards of ten colors, nearly all contain seals (vexillologists refer to these flags as SOBs: "Seals on Bedsheets"), and when placed together, they're hard to distinguish – case in point, check out the flags of 23 different US States in the image below:

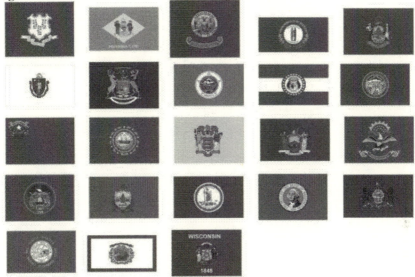

The above image is how the flags appear from a distance. Compare these "seals on a bedsheet" designs to the US State flags that largely honor the 5 Basic Rules:

Because state flags are largely boring "seals on a bedsheet", individuals wishing to express state pride must instead turn to athletic logos for identification. Being a West Virginia native and Virginia resident, I have never seen the flag of West Virginia or Virginia on a bumper sticker or on the back window of someone's vehicle; however, I have seen several

"Flying WV" logos and Virginia Tech VT's.

On the other hand, the flag of Tennessee, Texas, South Carolina and Maryland finds its way onto everything associated with the state because they're incredibly great flags!

Bad flags force residents to rely on sports logos for identity, while great flags are used in the development of sports logos… check out these three NFL teams whose states have meaningful and highly symbolic looking flags:

Baltimore Ravens & Maryland Flag:

Tennessee Titans & Tennessee Flag:

Houston Texans & Texas Flag

"Spring Has Sprung"

With all of this being said, the question I'm left pondering is this: As Appalachian—Americans, one of the nation's largest people groups, why is it that we do not have a symbol, a banner, a flag?

Could we all agree on what the flag would be? After all, we do stretch from Northern Alabama to the Canadian border.

I've been pondering this thought for quite some time and though I'm certainly not a flag designer (and I am sure the below design will elicit criticism), here's the flag I developed (background color is off yellow, the trim, lettering and symbols are dark green):

Explanation of the Symbolism

Why the Arrowhead?
We must never forget that long before this land was our land or that of our ancestors, it belonged to native peoples who were both warriors and farmers. They lived off the land and knew more about nature than modern man could ever realize. Their tribes were many and often they warred with each other. We honor them all by placing the universal symbol of Native Americans at the top of the flag.

Why the Crossed Muskets?
From the very earliest of days when our ancestors crested the Blue Ridge and laid eyes upon the Appalachian Mountains, they had in their hands firearms, both for personal protection and for survival. The two crossed muskets symbolize that arms are used both for hunting and defense.

Why the Black Bear?
The mountains of Appalachia were once dominated by mountain lion, the Carolina Parakeet flew through the dense forest canopy and the American Chestnut flourished; however, each of these have all but disappeared. Yet, the Black Bear has remained and is even growing in population. He symbolizes the Appalachian wilderness and represents all wildlife, both past and present.

Why the "Appalachia"?
Rule #4 of *Good Flag, Bad Flag: How to Design a Great Flag*. Specifically states "Never use writing of any kind…" And it is for this very reason that we do! To be Appalachian means that from time to time one must break rules and it would seem only fitting if the very banner of Appalachia defies at least one of the rules.

Our Vision
Our vision is that the banner of Appalachia will serve as a commonly accepted and celebrated symbol of the Appalachian people and region. We imagine the banner flying alongside the American and state flags at courthouses in small towns throughout the region, in front yards of proud Appalachian—Americans and on the back windows of SUVs and pickup trucks.

Our ultimate vision is for the flag of Appalachia to serve as a uniting banner for the people who call this great region home, regardless of their state residency, religion, political views or even favorite collegiate sports team.

Learn More
To learn more about the Flag of Appalachia project, visit www.AppalachianMagazine.com/AppalachianFlag

"Spring Has Sprung"

Submission from 94-Year-Old Writer
Written by Roberta Lacey, LPN retired. Walton, New York
Roberta Lacey, 94-years-old, attends a local library writers' group
and has been writing many stories of life in quieter times.

All names and places fictionalized for privacy.

My first meeting with Elsie was shortly after her admission to Fairview nursing home.

She was tall, robust and appeared to be in good physical condition. I could hear her pleading with the nurse's aide to please shave off the fuzz on her chin. "My son is coming tomorrow" she was saying, "He's coming from Connecticut". "Can't do it now", one aide said; "maybe later"; "you'll have to wait for the next shift," said another, and so it went on through the day.

This wing at the home was a bit different from my previous wings which were considered "skilled" nursing. Those patients were the elderly sick, with sadly, an occasional young paraplegic or quadriplegic among the group of weathered souls.

Finally, seeing Elsie still had her fuzzy chin and slight mustache, I locked my medicine cart on wheels, acquired a razor and went to work. The smile on her face was well worth the time. Then, Elsie accepted her medicine gratefully. One would not easily guess she suffered from Alzheimer's.

Elsie's son reported upon her admission day, that his mother's illness manifested itself about a year ago when Elsie was only fifty-seven years old. Most of the time she was completely lucid, however, on occasion her forgetfulness was very recognizable. Elsie used to be sharp, remembered everything and prided herself for that. Sometimes her son would find her softly crying because she was beginning to know something was very wrong..."what is happening to me?" she asked. She was tested and on that sad day, found out what was wrong. She accepted the news but felt numb upon hearing the name "Alzheimer's". There must be some mistake, she thought, but very slowly the dreaded name left her memory and she seemed reasonably at peace.

Since the doctor at the nursing home prescribed two ounces of wine HS, PRN (at hours of sleep as is needed), I poured out her wine and she usually went to sleep shortly after. Elsie most often reminded me to give it to her. On one occasion she asked for more wine. "I spilled it" she said. Upon looking about the room and on her night dress, I found no wine stains. I allowed her to think how clever she was and poured out two teaspoonfuls of wine into her cup. I had to give her credit for trying to put one over on me. However when she saw the tiny amount I gave her, she probably wondered if I knew what she was up to. She made no complaint.

Elsie would have some very lucid moments. In fact, when she was dressed up in the afternoon, one would assume she was visiting one of the patients on that wing.

Elsie's niece came every Wednesday evening to take her to Bingo at a nearby Vet's club. Oh, how Elsie looked forward to that! After dinner and after her meds were given, she took her niece's arm and off they went.

As time went on, Elsie had fewer lucid moments. On occasion, I would see and hear her having the most pleasant conversation with her new found friend. Her friend looked exactly like Elsie, nodding her head in agreement with her as they stood in the hallway at night. The wide glass windows separated the blackness of the outdoors and the hallway lighting above Elsie's head. When Elsie was escorted back to her room, she said "goodbye" to her friend; Reflection was her name.

Elsie's condition now made it impossible for her to attend Bingo with her niece. Her lucid moments were few and far between. However, one night about ten P.M. Elsie was seen trotting down the hallway fully dressed. The nurse's aide thought she was asleep and left her guard post.

I say Elsie was fully dressed, however she put her clothing on in reverse. Her pretty dress was next to her skin, a petticoat on top of that, a brassiere came last, a pretty necklace dangled from her neck. She wore no stockings but wore her best shoes. With a hat on her head, handbag strap hanging from her arm, white dress gloves, she walked with purpose. I guess it was easy for her to figure out where to put the ten fingers.

Fortunately, an alarm went off upon reaching a certain threshold! "Where are you going?" asked an aide. "Bingo", answered Elsie. As she was escorted back to her room without too much resistance, it was explained to her that there was no Bingo that night.

Months went by, some uneventful, others unpredictable. Elsie was often in a world of her own. Her speech was garbled. At times she was very pleasant while repeating the same sounds over and over again. Other times she could be nasty and very resentful of the aides who would not allow her to enter other patient's rooms. Elsie loved to wander into any room she chose; picking up whatever she imagined belonged to her.

She brought all her treasures back to her own room when she was guided back by a nurse's aide. Of course the aide returned the loot to the proper owner after Elsie was put back to bed. There were many times when the owners of the treasures screamed for help, raising quite an uproar. Elsie truly believed this big house was her own and she allowed other people to live there too. Elsie could be vicious at times. She snuck up on an aide who had her back turned and gave the aide a good pounding.

One winter Elsie caught a heavy cold. She was treated by the physician, however bronchitis developed. Elsie was turned and repositioned regularly. She sat up-right as best she could for breathing exercises in the chair by a sun filled window on nice days.

Elsie was sent to the nearby hospital as the bronchitis developed into pneumonia; antibiotics were given, however she did not improve. When she refused food, IV fluids were given. When Elsie tried repeatedly to pull the IV tubing from her arm when she awakened, a gastric tube was finally inserted. To avoid bed sores Elsie was turned from side to side, her bed was at a 45 degree angle. Oxygen was given. I learned this from hospital reports.

All Elsie wanted to do was sleep away the hours whether being bathed, in bed or sitting in the chair. She did not appear to recognize anyone in her sleepy haze. Her eyes stared blankly, not responding to verbal stimuli. Her family and minister gathered around her bed.

One very early morning Elsie did respond. Her response was to God's call and went to Him in peace. Elsie died with dignity. She had been a fine lady.

An anonymous poet wrote a poem "What do you see, nurse?' I'll quote one line; "I'm an old lady now and nature is cruel; 'tis her jest to make old age look like a fool".

Poetry from the Carolina Mountains

Written by Anna Chastain

Anna is a native of the South Carolina mountains where she is continuously inspired by the beauty and culture of the Southern Appalachian Mountains. When she's not working or writing, you can probably find her wandering on a hiking trail somewhere in South Carolina or Western North Carolina.

<u>A Nighttime Drive</u>
Break away to breathe
the brisk, pure air
of high country.

Meander mindlessly,
somewhat spontaneously,
through the thick forest
on a road that snakes
in seamless switchbacks
to the top
of a hill.

Night hushes
a silent, sleepy landscape
into a dusky drowse.

The harsh, hurried glow
of an incandescent city
-fades away.

Look above.

The Milky Way,
no longer cloaked with human glow,
sparkles simply,
yet magnificently,
in marvelous manifestation
against a bold
backdrop
of black.

<u>Sunday Lunch</u>
Nostalgia
lends a lingering hand
to warm memories.

The calamitous chaos of
cousins at play
and the soul-satisfying smell
of a lovingly prepared potluck
fill four walls with
contented smiles.

Present eyes glance
around a filled table,
once declared as that of
'the kids',
smiles are shared and
memories retold with
resounding merriment.

Together, all is well.

<u>Subdivisions</u>
"It's progress," they say.
"We're being put on the map"-

As the timbered trees cry,
caught in the progress trap.

"There's much to celebrate,
notoriety to gain."
But first, pave the Earth
and numb her with chains.

"It will bring in jobs,
this is good for the locals."
Just ignore their accents
if they're too vocal.

"We've got to stay relevant
in this new age."
Give them subdivisions,
make them disengage.

High Holidays
Though the Lord is in your heart
he would like you to attend
a Sunday or two, sit in the pew
and talk to your old friend.

Oh, those unexpected times
when there comes a holy pull,
your heart, it tilts, with a twinge of guilt
no longer feeling full.

In the Spring we come to sing
about the resurrection,
sigh and smile, cling a while
to holy protection.

Winter whispers solemnly
in a newly quiet Earth,
and all is bright in Advent light
when angels sing of birth.

The hymnals lie there dusty
with their friend, the lonely pew,
waiting to share another prayer
with souls who need renewed.

If this Old House Could Talk: The Henry Jackson Homestead in Upshur County, W.Va.

Written by Melissa Ireland

Henry Jackson was the great-uncle of the Confederate General Stonewall Jackson, but was prominent in his own right in the era he lived. The homestead has been restored and maintained by Doug and Ann Livingston Bush, whose efforts are outlined in the text of the article.

Melissa Ireland serves as a freelance writer and works as a professional abstractor and freelance paralegal for a living, but loves to write articles on West Virginia history and people who live there. Her writing takes place in her cabin on the beautiful Buckhannon River in Barbour County, West Virginia, where her ancestors came over two hundred years ago to settle.

Photo submitted by Melissa Ireland

If an old house could talk, then the one standing on a small knoll in southeastern Upshur County belonging to Doug and Ann Livingston Bush would have so many stories to tell about the lives of the Henry Jackson family that lived there for two hundred years.

Henry Jackson was the youngest son of John Jackson and Elizabeth Cummins Jackson, born on July 10, 1774 on Turkey Run near Buckhannon two years before Independence. His life would begin and end a few miles apart on the Buckhannon River. Henry's life from the beginning would be surrounded with danger, excitement and chance. He spent his life on a farm that he loved alongside his large family, contributing to his community and praising God.

John Jackson, born in County Londonderry, Ireland had immigrated to the American colonies as a young man. Jackson family lore states that Elizabeth Cummins of London, England, was traveling on the same ship. The couple married in 1855 in Maryland then traveled west, first to Hampshire County before moving their family across the Appalachian Mountains to settle near the site of present-day Buckhannon where Elizabeth had obtained a patent for 3,000 acres.

In the year prior to moving permanently to the area, John and his sons Edward and George had traveled to Upshur County in the company of John Pringle and Samuel Pringle, brothers who had deserted their post in 1761 during the French and Indian War, and found refuge in the hollow of a large sycamore tree on the Buckhannon River. The Pringles hid out for about three years before running out of supplies. John Pringle journeyed to the South Branch River settlements in Hampshire County where he discovered that he and his brother were no longer wanted men. Later, they led a contingent of settlers back to Upshur County, including the Jacksons, who cleared some ground for crops and a homestead.

John Jackson and his sons George and Edward served as soldiers in the Revolutionary War.

During the war, Elizabeth Cummins Jackson took command of the homeplace which became known as "Jackson's Fort" where refugees could gather during the frequent Indian raids while the men were away. It was said of her "though a woman, had the stomach and mettle of a man and rendered valuable service by aiding and inspiring the resistance of the defenders." Elizabeth has been described in various accounts has having been an imposing and intelligent woman of tall stature and beauty.

After the war, life on the frontier began to reshape itself from settlements to communities.

John Jackson would become the first postmaster of the county in 1804. Part of Elizabeth's 3000 acre patent became the city of Buckhannon. Later, John and Elizabeth would move to Clarksburg, where they both died. Their children carved lives for themselves.

George Jackson became a captain in the military guard, served with George Rogers Clark, was a prominent member and three-term congressman of the Virginia Assembly, organized the first militia unit in 1779 in Upshur County and became a lawyer. John Jackson, Jr. dug a mill race creating the island in Buckhannon where he built a fine stone home. Colonel Edward Jackson was the first surveyor in Randolph County, built Jackson's Mill on the West Fork River in Lewis County, and was the grandfather of the famous Confederate General Thomas "Stonewall" Jackson.

In 1800, Henry Jackson married Mary Elizabeth Hyre, daughter of Jacob Hyre and Elizabeth Powers, pioneer settlers of Upshur County. Henry and Mary built their cabin near the Buckhannon River where they farmed large tracts. Over the next thirty-five years, before her death in 1835 at age 51, Mary gave birth to thirteen children: Ester Jackson, Elizabeth Permelia Pribble, William Vandevater Jackson, Hyre Jackson, Edward Cummins Jackson, Mary "Mariah" Jackson, Henry Jackson Jr., Amanda Melvina Pribble, Rachel Cecelia Miller, John Henderson Brake Jackson, Jacob Jackson, Ulysses Jackson and Mary Sophia Wyrick.

After Mary Jackson's death, Henry married his second wife Elizabeth "Betsy" Shreve in 1836, twenty-three-year-old daughter of Joseph Shreve and Elizabeth Brake. Henry, age sixty-two, was almost forty years Betsy's senior. Henry sired ten more children by Betsy: Decatur Jackson, Samuel Dexter Jackson, James H. Alonzo Jackson, Marion Orlando Jackson, Melissa Lowe, Columbia Roxanna Jackson, George Washington Jackson, Artimisha Marteney, Eclipso Mero Jackson and Gideon Draper Camden Jackson.

Henry followed in his brother Edward's footsteps by becoming a surveyor. Years later, his field notes would be used for arguments before the West Virginia Supreme Court in Rich vs. Braxton which held that fraudulent tax sales had taken place for contiguous lands under various

Commonwealth of Virginia patents and surveys.

Henry also was instrumental in securing a 35,000 acres survey project known as the Banks Survey to be laid out in 5,000-acre tracts, close to the end of Indian hostilities in West Virginia. It was named for Henry Banks, of the firm Hunter, Banks and Company, located in Richmond who claimed thousands of acres through military land warrants in return for merchandise supplied to Virginia during the Revolutionary War. Although he started it, Henry never completed the survey because of Indian raiding parties in the area. One of his crew members was the great Indian fighter Jesse Hughes, who had been hired as a hunter. Years later, when the survey was finally completed by other parties, it became the property of Lewis Maxwell, a noted land speculator and lawyer who became embroiled in a court battle to have it recognized as a legitimate survey to no avail.

An occurrence that has become a legend in West Virginia folklore took place during one of Henry's surveying forays into the wilderness. In the autumn of 1795, Henry was surveying near

the Holly River and Elk River watersheds of present-day Webster County, when one of his crew, a man named William Strange was instructed to take his pack horse over the mountain to the point of the Elk near the Carpenter Settlement. Strange failed to turn up for the agreed rendezvous the next morning and despite concentrated efforts by the surveying party, only his horse was located.

In 1835, forty years after disappearing William Strange's skeleton was discovered by hunters on the south side of the Elk River at the foot of a large tree. His rifle, shot pouch and powder horn were by his side. In the bark of the tree according to various tales, Strange had carved the words "Strange is my name, and I'm on a strange ground, and strange it is that I can't be found." Strange Creek near Clay County was named in his honor.

According to some accounts, while on a surveying trip in Braxton County, a man named Loudin, one of Henry Jackson's hunting party crew, killed a buffalo cow who was so old and tough that the men declared her to be "the granny of all buffaloes." Hence the name Granny's Creek.

Henry Jackson was known to have been a kind and compassionate man. Such was the case in point during an ejectment suit in Upshur County to remove Henry Colerider from his property.

Colerider was quoted as saying "Jackson, you have gained your suit, but I am penniless, I don't know what to do" to which Henry was said to have replied "Colerider, I pity. Give me your horse, and I will recover your land."

So much heartache must have been felt in the Jackson cabin over the years along with joyous occasions. Sadly, like so many frontier families, Henry not only buried his first wife Mary before his death at age seventy-eight on February 24, 1852, but had to endure the untimely deaths of Ester, Edward Cummins, Mariah, Jacob, Columbia Roxanna, and Eclipso Mero.

Ester Jackson never married and died at age thirty-four a short time after her mother's death. Edward Cummins Jackson, who was described as "slow witted" was killed by Indians in 1851 while crossing the western plains on the Oregon Trail with his sister Rebecca Miller and husband Lewis. Jacob, Eclipso, Mariah and Columbia Jackson died as infants.

Several of the Jackson children did not live to see ripe old age, dying soon after their father.

Decatur Jackson drowned as a young man of twenty-five. James H. Alonzo Jackson died at age twenty-four during the last years of the Civil War at Harper's Ferry. Melissa Jackson died at age eighteen of consumption soon after marrying James R. Lowe. George Washington Jackson died at age eight from typhoid fever.

Quite a few of Henry's children moved west in search of a better life. John Henderson Brake Jackson left home early and died at age forty-nine on his farmstead near West Union, Oregon. Of John, his father was have said to remarked of his burning ambitions "that he was acting unwisely...that he was pouring out of the bunghole and putting in with a spigot."

Ulysses who became a large landowner and served as a county commissioner in Washington County, Oregon, died at age fifty-eight. William Vandevater Jackson lived in West Union, Oregon where he farmed, living to be age sixty-six.

Rachel Jackson Miller made it to Woodland, Oregon after the Indian attack that took her brother, where she and her husband Lewis farmed before she divorced him in later years. Hyre Jackson became a lawyer and judge, settling near his siblings in Oregon where he died in 1873.

Mary Sophia Jackson Wyrick relocated to Dubuque County, Iowa where she and her husband farmed. Her sister Artimisha Jackson Marteney settled in Kingman County, Kansas.

Henry Jackson's will probated in 1851 in Upshur County supplied the information that he was a slave owner. As a practicing Universalist, Henry avowed his faith in his last words "I commit my body to the ground, and my soul to God who gave it, having no doubt that he will take care of all his creatures." Universalism was a common theological belief held in Henry's time that Jesus had died for all the sins of man, and that all men would eventually see heaven. The will also gleaned the fact that Henry was embroiled in several lawsuits to which he instructed his wife to continue. Elizabeth was given the whole of his lands and property, save for some bequests to his daughters, for as long as she remained his widow.

Henry Jackson was laid to rest in the family cemetery overlooking his homeplace. The final resting place of his wife and him are marked by unique coffin shaped tombstones, which were pulled in place by teams of oxen.

In 1868, the lands of Henry Jackson were partitioned among his heirs. His son Samuel Dexter Jackson received the portion of the farm where the cabin stood and the family cemetery.

Samuel Dexter, born in 1838, married Martha Elizabeth Marple, daughter of Moses Marple and Elizabeth Bennett of Peck's Run in Upshur County in 1861 at the beginning of the Civil War.

Interesting enough, although Henry Jackson was a slave owner, his sons Samuel Dexter, Marion Orlando and James Alonzo enlisted in the Union side by joining Co. H of the 3rd West Virginia Calvary Regiment during the war, where they served under Colonel David Hunter Strother.

Strother was better known under his pseudonym Porte Crayon, and was a famous writer and illustrator, born in Martinsburg, West Virginia. The 3rd West Virginia Calvary Regiment fought in the battles of Bull Run, Moorefield and Droop Mountain, and participated in General Philip H. Sheridan's Virginia campaign. The regiment was also present at Appomattox when General Robert E. Lee surrendered. The regiment is memorialized at Gettysburg where a marker is inscribed with the words "Erected by the State of West Virginia to commemorate the valor and fidelity of the Third West Virginia Calvary."

Pictures of Samuel in his military uniform shows a handsome man with a shock of dark hair and full beard staring solemnly with a direct gaze. His wife Martha appears in photographs as a black hair beauty, seemingly petite. Samuel and Martha lived in the original Henry Jackson cabin, built "Yankee "style in the early 1800s on a 16 foot by 16-foot stone foundation, which featured hand-hewn chestnut beams and pegged framing. The small cabin contained a loft and was anchored by a large hand-cut stone fireplace. At the time Henry Jackson built the structure, nails had to be made individually by a blacksmith which were costly and hard to come by. A "Yankee' frame house had no nails and was put together with pegs.

Around 1890, Samuel Dexter Jackson expanded the cabin by adding an addition to the side and a second story for his growing family. John, the first son of Samuel and Martha died at age two, but they were blessed with a second son in 1866 and named him Marion Columbus Jackson.

Nine more children would follow: Ulysses Grant Jackson, Anna Myrtle Jackson, Granville Dexter Jackson, Clipso Elizabeth Barbe, Henrietta Arizona Newcomb, Mary Esta Loudin, Roscoe Conklin Jackson, Bernard Leo Jackson and Franklin Claude Jackson.

Samuel Dexter Jackson died in 1911 at age seventy-two; Martha followed in 1914. Both were laid to rest in the family cemetery. Samuel's obituary extolled the fact that he had been one of the oldest settlers in Upshur County and that his last words before death had been "I now see the King that owns all the land." Samuel & Martha's son Roscoe Conklin Jackson was the next generation of the Jackson family to live in the family homestead.

Roscoe "Rossie" Jackson was born in 1882 the ninth child of Samuel and Martha Jackson.

In 1916, he married Lena Madge Radabaugh, a local girl who was a daughter of Bezalee Radabaugh and Florence Ann Brown. Roscoe and Madge were in their thirties when they married and set up housekeeping on the Jackson homestead. On his WWI draft card registration, Roscoe is described as being of medium build with blue eyes and brown hair.

Timbering and farming supported Roscoe and Madge all the years they spent together.

Soon after their marriage, they welcomed daughter Martha Irene in 1918. Their son Theodore "Ted" Lester Jackson arrived in 1923. Roscoe's brothers Claude and Bernard lived on the farm with them for several years.

In 1922, the Jackson Family Association was formed to serve as a reunion for descendants of John Jackson and Elizabeth Cummins Jackson to preserve heritage and family ties. Roscoe's family was often in attendance at Jackson's Mill until the gathering ceased meeting in 1941 at the beginning of WWII. The Jackson Brigade Association now continues to act as the official genealogy society for the descendants of John Jackson and is the source for much of the Jackson family information contained herein.

"Spring Has Sprung"

In 1937, a happy event occurred in the Roscoe's family when Martha Irene Jackson married Burl Gillum a few weeks before Christmas. Son Theodore attended nearby Wesleyan College for a year before enlisting in 1943 in the Army.

Roscoe Jackson contracted influenza in the fall of 1959 at age seventy-seven and died of a heart attack from complications. Instead of being buried in the Jackson family cemetery, he was interred nearby at Heavner Cemetery at Buckhannon. Madge lived until 1967, moving off the homestead to Roanoke, Virginia to be near her daughter and son.

In 1986, over two hundred years after Henry Jackson's birth, and after acquiring other Jackson heirs' interests, Martha Irene Jackson Gillum and Theodore Lester Jackson sold the farm to a private individual, thus ending two centuries of Jackson family ownership of the cabin and land that it stands on.

Doug Bush and Ann Livingston Bush purchased the Jackson homestead in 1993. At the time, the house had been neglected for several years, but the original cabin and stone fireplace were intact. Many years later after a prolonged labor of love, the house has been restored to the beautiful edifice it is now. The farm and rolling hayfields sustain the Bush family much as it did the Jackson family over the course of two centuries. Doug is a retired history teacher and coach and now serves as the supervisor of the Tygarts Valley Conservation District and is a member of the West Virginia Farm Bureau. Ann has spent her career in the insurance business. Both are immensely happy in being stewards of the Jackson farm and look forward to passing the farm on to their daughters and families.

Henry Jackson's life accomplishments might seem small in comparison with the many contributions made by his prominent family, but it is evident that the most important achievement that he was most proud of was raising his large family. Henry must have been satisfied that he had been born in the wilderness, lived in the Virginia colony that became a state, resided in Randolph County which later gave birth to Upshur County, and never had to leave his chair in front of his fireplace that was so well built that it is enjoyed still today. He truly exemplified the pioneer spirit.

What did you think? We'd love to hear from you!
Send us an email at the following address:

TheMountainWriter@gmail.com

"Spring Has Sprung"

Wishing you and your family a Happy Spring.

Thank you for subscribing to **Appalachian Magazine!**

Visit:
AppalachianMagazineStore.com
to purchase a subscription today!

Made in the USA
Columbia, SC
25 March 2020